Acknowledgments

This edition grew out of a process that began over three years ago. At that time, we convened a group of colleagues to help us determine how best to support teachers in understanding and applying *The Creative Curriculum*'s child development goals and objectives. The first step was to review national and state standards in each of the disciplines, revise the goals and objectives of *The Creative Curriculum*, and create the Developmental Continuum. We are indebted to Dr. Carol Copple, who took a lead role in this effort and continued to review and help us refine subsequent drafts. Derry G. Koralek, Monica Vacca, and Elizabeth Servideo also provided invaluable assistance in this task. We owe a very special acknowledgment to Whit Hayslip, coordinator of Infant and Preschool Programs, Division of Special Education, in the Los Angeles Unified School District. As part of the district's professional development program, he and Karen Krische, program specialist, arranged for a group of special education preschool teachers to work on the Continuum with Dr. M. Diane Klein, chair of the Special Education Division at California State University, Los Angeles. This group of teachers developed the Forerunners, piloted the instrument in their classrooms, and generously shared their experiences.

When we completed the first draft, we asked several colleagues to review it critically and give us suggestions for improving the document. Their very helpful feedback helped us to shape this new resource. We particularly want to thank Dr. Sue Bredekamp, Dr. Cindy Elliott, Gaye Gronlund, Whit Hayslip, Candy Jones, Trudi Norman-Murch, Charlotte Stetson, Monica Vacca, and Sallie Van Avery for generously giving us their time and recommendations. We greatly appreciate the feedback we received from Jan Whitney, Marilyn Box, and the Mesa Early Learning Preschool teachers in Mesa, Arizona, who field tested the Continuum.

Special thanks go to Toni Bickart, who read many drafts, challenged us to think more deeply about several topics, and gave us numerous suggestions. We also thank Emily Kohn, our invaluable content editor; Jean Bernard, our meticulous copy editor; Carla Uriona for production of the new edition; and Douglas Gritzmacher for the cover design.

Connecting Content, Teaching, and Learning

Revised Edition

Diane Trister Dodge ❀ Laura J. Colker ❀ Cate Heroman

Washington, DC

Editor: Emily Kohn
Cover Design: Douglas Gritzmacher

Copyright © 2000, 2002 by Teaching Strategies, Inc.
All rights reserved. No part of this book may be reproduced in any form or by any electronic
or mechanical means, including information storage and retrieval systems—except in the
case of brief quotations embodied in critical articles or reviews—without prior written
permission from Teaching Strategies, Inc.

Published by:
Teaching Strategies, Inc.
P.O. Box 42243
Washington, DC 20015
www.TeachingStrategies.com

Originally published: 2000
1st revised edition printing: 2002

ISBN 1-879537-70-2

Teaching Strategies and *The Creative Curriculum* names and logos are
registered trademarks of Teaching Strategies, Inc., Washington, DC.

Table of Contents

Introduction

How do you know if your program is effective and whether children are learning? What kinds of experiences should children have during their early years that will help them develop the skills and motivation they need to become lifelong learners? How do teachers address content appropriately in a *Creative Curriculum* classroom?

Since publication of the third edition of *The Creative Curriculum*, we have worked with teachers in a wide range of programs, helping them to answer these questions. In doing so, we have examined new research on brain development and best practices, read state-of-the-art reports on teaching and learning, and studied content standards developed by states and professional organizations since *The Creative Curriculum*'s publication.

While these efforts continue to confirm the value of *The Creative Curriculum*'s environmentally based approach, we feel that more clarity would enhance teachers' effectiveness in understanding how content is linked to teaching and learning in a developmentally appropriate curriculum. The purpose of this supplement, therefore, is to explain these relationships.

In addition, all of us must take seriously the increasing emphasis on academics, standards, and accountability and respond appropriately and with integrity. Therefore, a second purpose of this book is to explain how and what children are learning to those who want and need reassurance—parents, administrators, funders, and the public. We want to offer users of *The Creative Curriculum* specific guidance on how to effectively address content within our *Curriculum* framework and how to ensure that every child is developing and learning. This resource, *Connecting Content, Teaching, and Learning*, contains the following:

Chapter I, Curriculum Goals and Objectives, shows what growth to expect in children ages 3 to 5, including those who may not be at a typical level of development.

Chapter II, What Children Learn—The Content of the Curriculum, provides an overview of key components of national and state standards in each subject area—literacy, math, science, social studies, the arts, and technology. We illustrate the connection between content learning and our goals and objectives, and give examples of how teachers promote learning in the context of everyday classroom experiences.

Chapter III, **Returning to the Curriculum,** brings the focus back to an environmental approach. As a teacher, you are responsible for implementing curriculum and guiding children's learning. *The Creative Curriculum* offers many concrete ideas on how to set up an environment and help children learn. In this chapter we revisit how teachers use interest areas and studies to promote learning, and how they individualize the *Curriculum*.

The **Appendices** contain a copy of the Goals and Objectives at a Glance, *The Creative Curriculum®* Developmental Continuum, more detailed information on gross motor development, and a Child Progress and Planning Report. In the appendices you will also find a series of charts for each of the content areas. These charts enable you to align the requirements for your program with content standards and *The Creative Curriculum.* They present the key components of each content area, identify *Curriculum* goals and objectives that relate to each component, and provide a column where you can list the requirements that apply to your program.

Connecting Content, Teaching, and Learning describes the central role of teachers in an environmentally based, interactive, play-oriented curriculum where children master important skills and content and develop social competence. We strongly believe that teachers who understand the developmental steps in each objective can support learning and convey content in appropriate ways. Teachers don't have to choose between an academic approach and play. Just as a jigsaw puzzle fits together once you figure out where the pieces go, we hope this book will help you create your own picture of how to connect content, teaching, and learning as you implement *The Creative Curriculum.*

What Children Learn in *The Creative Curriculum®*

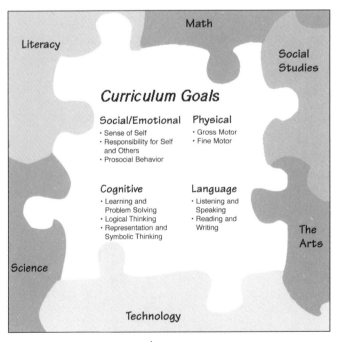

Chapter I
Curriculum Goals and Objectives

Goals and objectives are the road map of an early childhood curriculum. They give you a direction for planning your program and a way to determine what children know and how they are developing. This information enables you to respond to each child individually, to build on strengths and target skills that need strengthening.[1] Just as you interpret any road map, you have to be familiar with the signs along the way and you must have a good idea of where you are heading. Goals and objectives can point you in the right direction and offer routes that are both interesting and enriching.

Because early childhood teachers focus on "the whole child" to promote learning, the goals of an early childhood curriculum should focus on all aspects of development:

* *Social/Emotional Development:* children's feelings about themselves, the development of responsibility, and their ability to relate positively to others.
* *Physical Development:* children's gross and fine motor development.
* *Cognitive Development:* children's thinking skills, including the development of symbolic and problem-solving skills.
* *Language Development:* children's ability to communicate through words, both spoken and written.

On the next two pages, we present *The Creative Curriculum* goals and objectives. To highlight how all areas of development are interrelated, think about how teachers help preschool children continue their steps toward becoming readers. Teachers use every opportunity to expose children to new words and to help children learn that print conveys a message (language goals). They select books that reflect the children's backgrounds and interests and display them throughout the classroom so children can use them independently and cooperatively (social and emotional goals). To help children develop the small muscle control necessary to hold books properly and turn pages, teachers provide interlocking toys, scissors, and writing tools for children to use (physical development). And to help children develop symbolic thinking skills, teachers encourage children to act out stories (cognitive development).

---

[1] Our colleague, Judy Jablon, gave us this way of discussing children's needs. We find it much more positive than the deficit approach that often permeates our language in describing children.

The Creative Curriculum

SOCIAL/EMOTIONAL DEVELOPMENT

Sense of Self

1. Shows ability to adjust to new situations
2. Demonstrates appropriate trust in adults
3. Recognizes own feelings and manages them appropriately
4. Stands up for rights

Responsibility for Self and Others

5. Demonstrates self-direction and independence
6. Takes responsibility for own well-being
7. Respects and cares for classroom environment and materials
8. Follows classroom routines
9. Follows classroom rules

Prosocial Behavior

10. Plays well with other children
11. Recognizes the feelings of others and responds appropriately
12. Shares and respects the rights of others
13. Uses thinking skills to resolve conflicts

PHYSICAL DEVELOPMENT

Gross Motor

14. Demonstrates basic locomotor skills (running, jumping, hopping, galloping)
15. Shows balance while moving
16. Climbs up and down
17. Pedals and steers a tricycle (or other wheeled vehicle)
18. Demonstrates throwing, kicking, and catching skills

Fine Motor

19. Controls small muscles in hands
20. Coordinates eye-hand movement
21. Uses tools for writing and drawing

Goals and Objectives

COGNITIVE DEVELOPMENT

Learning and Problem Solving

22. Observes objects and events with curiosity
23. Approaches problems flexibly
24. Shows persistence in approaching tasks
25. Explores cause and effect
26. Applies knowledge or experience to a new context

Logical Thinking

27. Classifies objects
28. Compares/measures
29. Arranges objects in a series
30. Recognizes patterns and can repeat them
31. Shows awareness of time concepts and sequence
32. Shows awareness of position in space
33. Uses one-to-one correspondence
34. Uses numbers and counting

Representation and Symbolic Thinking

35. Takes on pretend roles and situations
36. Makes believe with objects
37. Makes and interprets representations

LANGUAGE DEVELOPMENT

Listening and Speaking

38. Hears and discriminates the sounds of language
39. Expresses self using words and expanded sentences
40. Understands and follows oral directions
41. Answers questions
42. Asks questions
43. Actively participates in conversations

Reading and Writing

44. Enjoys and values reading
45. Demonstrates understanding of print concepts
46. Demonstrates knowledge of the alphabet
47. Uses emerging reading skills to make meaning from print
48. Comprehends and interprets meaning from books and other texts
49. Understands the purpose of writing
50. Writes letters and words

Looking at Goals and Objectives on a Continuum

Children don't accomplish a particular skill all at once. Rather, they progress through a sequence of steps. Having a way to determine where each child is in relation to curriculum goals and objectives allows you to decide what specific support and what kinds of experiences will enable every child to develop and learn.

The Creative Curriculum Developmental Continuum is a tool that gives you a broad picture of what development for 3- to 5-year-olds looks like for each of the *Curriculum* objectives. The figure below illustrates the different components of the Continuum.

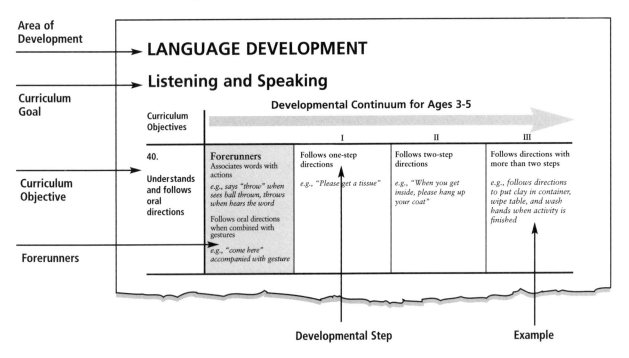

The three non-shaded boxes below the long gray arrow (labeled steps I, II, and III) represent the expected developmental steps in the preschool years (children ages 3 to 5). Each box describes a particular point in skill development. Because children develop at very different rates, these boxes do **not** represent a specific age; rather, they show the expected **developmental steps** in mastering the objective. Step I, therefore, approximates a beginning level of development. For objective 40, "Understands and follows oral directions," step I reads "Follows one-step directions." To give you a picture of what this might look like in real life, we provide an **example:** *Please get a tissue.*

In step II, we offer the next level in acquiring this skill: "Follows two-step directions given." An example might be a child who can carry out this oral direction: *When you get inside, please hang up your coat.*

4

Step III represents a higher level of skill development: "Follows directions with more than two steps." An example that illustrates this step is, *Follows directions to put clay in container, wipe table, and wash hands when activity is finished.*

Keep in mind that because all of the examples presented in the Continuum are *sample* behaviors, you may or may not observe these actual behaviors. Children demonstrate their mastery of skills in a variety of ways.

Including All Children

The skills and stages identified in steps I, II, and III will describe most of the children in your program. However, there is a range of development in any group of young children. You will probably have children in your program whose development in one or more areas may not be typical. Some of these children may have special education needs. Indeed, with the emphasis in federal law on educating children in the "least restrictive environment" (as mandated by the Individuals with Disabilities Education Act), more children with disabilities are joining their non-disabled peers in preschool.

Because *The Creative Curriculum* is designed to meet the needs of all preschool children—not just those experiencing typical development—the Continuum gives you a way of identifying children who are not yet at the beginning level of typical preschool development, as indicated by Step I. These children, however, are showing beginning evidence of developing the requisite skills and knowledge involved—a strength on which you can build. What we have done in the shaded box, therefore, is to offer some possible **forerunner** skills. In the example we've been using (Objective 40, "Understands and follows oral directions"), forerunner skills include:

* Associates words with actions (*e.g., says "throw" when sees ball thrown, throws when hears the word*)
* Follows oral directions when combined with gestures (*e.g., "come here" accompanied by gesture*)

These are examples of the many possible forerunner skills a child in your program might exhibit. Before achieving a skill that is typical of 3- to 5-year-olds, children with delays will display a wide range of emerging behaviors. You are likely to observe forerunner skills that either precede or follow the ones we have included in the Continuum. The forerunners we list do not represent a timeline; they are offered as sample possible skills and behaviors on which you can build when planning for children.

The addition of this forerunner box supports a belief that underlies *The Creative Curriculum:* all children bring with them strengths and abilities on which you can build.

The Benefits of a Continuum

Here are some of the key ways in which *The Creative Curriculum* Developmental Continuum can become an invaluable tool for planning your program and individualizing the curriculum for each child.

❋ It breaks down each objective so you can have realistic expectations as you plan your program.

❋ It helps you observe and plan for *all* children in your program, including those who may not be developing typically, and note their progress over time.

❋ It fosters a positive approach to teaching—looking at what children *can* do and thinking about what comes next rather than documenting what they can't do.

❋ It gives you a wealth of information to share with families that will reassure them about their child's progress as a learner.

Below you will find the goals and objectives of *The Creative Curriculum* and the continuum of development for each one.

Social/Emotional Development

The preschool years are a prime time for developing social and emotional skills that are essential to children's well-being and success, in school and in life. With the current focus on readiness, accountability, and high standards, there is always a danger that programs will push inappropriate academic skills and ignore other aspects of development that encourage long-lasting and positive results.

Fortunately, we can rely on a substantial body of research that clearly demonstrates the connection between social and emotional competence and academic success.[2]

Children who are socially and emotionally ready for school are:

❋ confident, friendly, has developed or will be able to develop good relationships with peers;

❋ able to concentrate on and persist at challenging tasks;

❋ able to effectively communicate frustrations, anger, and joy; and

❋ able to listen to instructions and be attentive.

Strategies for achieving these social and emotional objectives are embedded throughout *The Creative Curriculum*. We have organized the objectives under three goals: sense of self, responsibility for self and others, and prosocial behavior.

---

[2] Pelligrini, A. D., and Carl D. Glickman. "Measuring Kindergartners' Social Competence." *ERIC Digest.* Urbana, IL: ERIC Clearinghouse on Elementary and Early Childhood Education, 1991.

Sense of Self

objective
1. Shows ability to adjust to new situations

	I	II	III
Forerunners Interacts with teachers when family member is nearby Is able to move away from family member; checks back occasionally ("social referencing")	Treats arrival and departure as routine parts of the day *e.g., says good-bye to family members without undue stress; accepts comfort from teacher*	Accepts changes in daily schedules and routines *e.g., eagerly participates in a field trip; accepts visitors to classroom*	Functions with increasing independence in school *e.g., readily goes to other parts of the building for scheduled activities; willingly delivers a message from classroom teacher to the office*

objective
2. Demonstrates appropriate trust in adults

	I	II	III
Forerunners Seeks to be near trusted adult as a "safe haven" Makes visual or physical contact with trusted adult for reassurance	Shows confidence in parents' and teachers' abilities to keep him/her safe and healthy *e.g., explores the indoor and outdoor environments without being fearful; summons adult when assistance is needed*	Regards parents and teachers as resources and positive role models *e.g., imitates parents going to work or at home during dramatic play; asks teacher's advice on how to saw a piece of wood in half*	Knows the difference between adults who can help (family members, friends, staff) and those who may not (strangers) *e.g., knows who is allowed to give her medicine; talks about why children shouldn't go anywhere with strangers*

objective
3. Recognizes own feelings and manages them appropriately

	I	II	III
Forerunners Cries to express displeasure Uses facial expressions to communicate feelings *e.g., nods when asked if he is feeling sad*	Identifies and labels own feelings *e.g., says, "I'm mad at you"; "I really want to paint today"*	Is able to describe feelings and their causes *e.g., says, "I'm excited because my dad is coming home"; "I'm mad because they won't let me play with them"*	Is increasingly able to manage own feelings *e.g., calms self down when angry and uses words to explain why; chooses to go to a quiet area to be alone when upset*

Sense of Self, continued

objective
4. Stands up for rights

	I	II	III
Forerunners Protests when slighted or wronged by crying or yelling Grabs or pushes when seeking a desired toy	Physically or verbally asserts needs and desires *e.g., continues to hold classroom pet another child wants; lets teacher know if another child refuses to give anyone a turn on the ride-on truck*	Asserts own needs and desires verbally without being aggressive *e.g., says, "It's my turn now" when sand timer runs out; tells friend who asks to paint at the easel, "I'm not done," and continues working*	Takes action to avoid possible disputes over rights *e.g., puts up "Do not knock down" sign in front of block structure; divides sandbox into area for himself and peer*

Responsibility for Self and Others

objective
5. Demonstrates self-direction and independence

	I	II	III
Forerunners Purposefully indicates needs or wants (may be nonverbal) Selects toy or activity; plays briefly	Chooses and becomes involved in one activity out of several options *e.g., during free play decides to play with giant dominoes on floor in toys and games area; after waking up from nap, takes book from shelf in library area and looks at it*	Completes multiple tasks in a project of own choosing with some adult assistance *e.g., makes a collage: collects materials, glue, paper, and scissors and works until done; builds a zoo with blocks, animal and people props, and cars*	Carves out and completes own task without adult assistance *e.g., draws one section of mural without intruding on other sections; makes a book about family trip that includes 5 pictures in sequence*

objective
6. Takes responsibility for own well-being

	I	II	III
Forerunners Allows adult to attend to personal needs such as dressing or washing hands without resistance Uses self-help skills with adult assistance such as brushing teeth or putting on coat with help	Uses self-help skills with occasional reminders *e.g., tries new foods when encouraged by teacher; washes hands with soap and water following procedures taught*	Uses self-help skills and participates in chores without reminders *e.g., goes to get a sponge after spilling juice; helps throw away trash after a picnic*	Understands the importance of self-help skills and their role in healthy living *e.g., tries new foods and talks about what's good for you; knows why it's important to wash hands and brush teeth*

8

Responsibility for Self and Others, continued

objective
7. Respects and cares for classroom environment and materials

	I	II	III
Forerunners Engages with/explores materials for brief periods of time with adult assistance or independently Participates in clean-up routines when asked	Uses materials in appropriate ways *e.g., paints at easel; turns pages in book carefully without tearing*	Puts away used materials before starting another activity *e.g., shuts off the tape recorder before leaving the listening center; returns puzzle to shelf*	Begins to take responsibility for care of the classroom environment *e.g., gets broom and dust pan to help remove sand; pitches in willingly to move furniture to clear a group area*

objective
8. Follows classroom routines

	I	II	III
Forerunners Allows adult to move him/her through routines Follows classroom routines with assistance such as reminders, picture cues, or physical help	Participates in classroom activities (e.g., circle time, clean-up, napping, toileting, eating, etc.) with prompting *e.g., after cleaning up, goes to rug for circle time when the teacher strums the autoharp*	Understands and follows classroom procedures without prompting *e.g., goes to wash hands and brush teeth after lunch*	Follows and understands the purpose of classroom procedures *e.g., tells peer that he can't eat lunch until he's washed his hands*

objective
9. Follows classroom rules

	I	II	III
Forerunners Follows simple directions and limits when told by an adult Follows classroom rules with assistance such as reminders, picture cues, or physical help	Follows classroom rules with reminders *e.g., responds positively to guidance such as "speak with your indoor voice"*	Understands and follows classroom rules without reminders *e.g., returns puzzles to shelf before leaving the table area*	Follows and understands reasons for classroom rules *e.g., tells friend to put artwork on shelf so it will be safe; reminds peer not to run in classroom so that no one will get hurt*

Prosocial Behavior

objective
10. Plays well with other children

I	II	III
Forerunners Tolerates being physically near others Plays alongside another child Enjoys simple back and forth games such as hide and seek	Works/plays cooperatively with one other child e.g., draws or paints beside peer, making occasional comments; has a pretend phone conversation with another child	Successfully enters a group and plays cooperatively e.g., joins other children caring for babies in dramatic play center; plans with peers what they will need to set up a class restaurant	Maintains an ongoing friendship with at least one other child e.g., says, "We're friends again, right?" after working through a conflict; talks about another child as "my best friend"

objective
11. Recognizes the feelings of others and responds appropriately

I	II	III
Forerunners Notices expressions of feelings in others e.g., looks or reacts by crying or laughing Imitates other children's expressions of feelings	Is aware of other children's feelings and often responds in a like manner e.g., laughs or smiles when others are happy; says a child is sad because her mom left	Shows increasing awareness that people may have different feelings about the same situation e.g., says that another child is afraid of thunder but, "I'm not"; acts out role of angry parent during pretend play	Recognizes what another person might need or want e.g., brings a book on trucks to show a child who loves trucks; helps a friend who is having difficulty opening a milk carton

objective
12. Shares and respects the rights of others

I	II	III
Forerunners Plays alongside another child using same or similar materials with adult assistance Plays alongside another child using same or similar materials without conflict	With prompts, shares or takes turns with others e.g., allows sand timer to regulate turns with favorite toys; complies with teacher's request to let another child have a turn on the tricycle	Shares toys or allows turn in response to another child's request e.g., appropriately occupies self while waiting for others to leave swings without crying or demanding a turn; plays at sand table without grabbing items being used by others	Shares and defends the rights of others to a turn e.g., reminds child who doesn't want to relinquish a turn that it is another child's turn; asks teacher to intervene when two children begin to fight over a toy

Prosocial Behavior, continued

objective

13. Uses thinking skills to resolve conflicts

	I	II	III
Forerunners Accepts adult solution to resolve a conflict Seeks adult assistance to resolve a conflict *e.g., cries, approaches adult, or asks for help*	Accepts compromise when suggested by peer or teacher *e.g., agrees to play with another toy while waiting for a turn; goes to "peace table" with teacher and peer to solve a problem*	Suggests a solution to solve a problem; seeks adult assistance when needed *e.g., suggests trading one toy for another; asks teacher to make a waiting list for the water table*	Engages in a process of negotiation to reach a compromise *e.g., works out roles for a dramatic play episode; suggests going to the "peace table" to work out a problem*

Physical Development

Children's physical development is sometimes taken for granted in early childhood. We assume children will progress though a predictable sequence of stages and acquire certain skills. However, physical development is far too important to leave to chance.

Physical skills are important in their own right and for future tasks in reading, writing, scientific exploration, and math. For example, when children string beads, line up shells, or use the zipper on a self-help frame, they are refining their eye-hand coordination, their fine motor skills, and their sense of directionality.

Physical development also affects social/emotional development. As children learn what their bodies can do, they gain self-confidence. The more they can do, the more willingly they try new and increasingly challenging tasks. This positive attitude means that children are more willing to try out new physical skills without fear of failure. This increased self-confidence positively influences their attitude toward learning in other areas of development as well.

The benefits of promoting physical skills are well documented. The Surgeon General's Report on Physical Activity and Health (1996) states that physical activity contributes significantly to personal health and well-being. Physical education in the early grades contributes to children's academic achievement, general health, self-esteem, stress management, and social development. And we know from brain research that movement literally "wakes up" the brain.

For these reasons, *The Creative Curriculum* goals and objectives guide teachers in providing opportunities each day for children to move skillfully, manipulate objects, balance and control their bodies, and refine small muscle skills. We have organized the objectives for physical development in two broad goals: gross motor and fine motor skills.

Gross Motor*

objective

14. Demonstrates basic locomotor skills (running, jumping, hopping, galloping)

I   II   III

Forerunners	Moves with direction and beginning coordination	Moves with direction and increasing coordination	Moves with direction and refined coordination
Walks with assistance Runs, sometimes falls Jumps and hops with hand held	*e.g., runs avoiding obstacles; jumps forward, may lead with one foot; hops in place once or twice*	*e.g., runs moving arms and legs; does a running jump with both feet; attempts to skip, often reverting to galloping*	*e.g., runs quickly changing directions, starting and stopping; jumps forward from standing position; gallops smoothly*

objective

15. Shows balance while moving

I   II   III

Forerunners	Attempts to walk along a line, stepping off occasionally	Walks along wide beam such as edge of sandbox	Walks forward easily, and backward with effort, along a wide beam
Walks on toes Easily stops, starts, changes direction, avoids obstacles Walks forward straddling line			

objective

16. Climbs up and down

I   II   III

Forerunners	Climbs a short, wide ladder	Climbs up and down stairs and ladders, and around obstacles	Climbs and plays easily on ramps, stairs, ladders, or sliding boards
Crawls up stairs on own Walks up stairs with hand held Climbs a short, wide ladder with support from adult			

* Teachers who work with children who may have developmental lags in gross motor skills will find it helpful to see the specific developmental steps for running, jumping, hopping, galloping, throwing, kicking, and catching. A breakdown of these gross motor skills appears in Appendix C.

Gross Motor, continued

objective
17. Pedals and steers a tricycle (or other wheeled vehicle)

	I	II	III
Forerunners Sits on tricycle or other riding toy, pushing forward/backward with feet not using pedals Pedals tricycle, difficulty with steering	Pedals in forward direction, steering around wide corners	Pedals and steers around obstacles and sharp corners	Rides with speed and control

objective
18. Demonstrates throwing, kicking, and catching skills

	I	II	III
Forerunners Hurls beanbag or ball Sits on floor and traps a rolled ball with arms and body Kicks a ball a short distance with hand held to maintain balance	Throws, catches, and kicks objects with somewhat awkward movements *e.g., throws ball with both hands; catches a large ball against body; kicks ball from standing position*	Throws, catches, and kicks with increasing control *e.g., throws ball overhand several feet toward target; catches bounced ball; moves toward ball and kicks*	Throws and kicks at target and catches with increasing accuracy *e.g., throws object with smooth overhand motion; catches object with elbows bent; kicks ball with fluid motion*

Fine Motor

objective
19. Controls small muscles in hands

	I	II	III
Forerunners Uses self-help skills such as: finger feeds self; removes shoes/socks; washes hands with assistance Drops objects into container Touches thumb to finger to pick up object	Manipulates objects with hands *e.g., places large pegs in pegboard; buttons large buttons on own clothes; uses scissors to make snips*	Manipulates smaller objects with increasing control *e.g., eats with a fork; inserts and removes small pegs in pegboard; squeezes clothespin to hang painting; cuts with scissors along a straight or slightly curved line*	Manipulates a variety of objects requiring increased coordination *e.g., creates recognizable objects with clay; buttons, zips, and sometimes ties; cuts with scissors along lines, turning corners; cuts simple shapes out of paper*

objective
20. Coordinates eye-hand movement

	I	II	III
Forerunners Removes pegs from pegboard Opens a board book and turns a page Puts one block on top of another, holding the base block	Performs simple manipulations *e.g., makes a necklace with a string and large beads; rolls and pounds playdough; places pegs in pegboard*	Performs simple manipulations with increasing control *e.g., makes a necklace using small beads; pours water into a funnel*	Manipulates materials in a purposeful way, planning and attending to detail *e.g., strings a variety of small objects (straws, buttons, etc.); using table blocks, creates a tall structure that balances; completes 8-piece puzzle*

objective
21. Uses tools for writing and drawing

	I	II	III
Forerunners Holds large writing tool and marks with it Holds marker in palmar grasp and scribbles	Holds a marker or crayon with thumb and two fingers; makes simple strokes	Makes several basic strokes or figures; draws some recognizable objects	Copies and draws simple shapes, letters, and words including name

Cognitive Development

Cognitive development is the process of learning to think and reason. Preschool-age children are developing cognitive skills that prepare them for content work in all disciplines. They are becoming skilled observers and questioners and are learning how to organize and represent new information.

In reviewing standards in the content areas, you will find a common thread that runs throughout. Cognitive or thinking skills are embedded within language and literacy, mathematics, science, social studies, the arts, and technology. Most standards documents refer to them as "process skills." As you read through the list of goals and objectives for cognitive development, think about how each might be applied in different academic areas. For example, the objective "explores cause and effect" can be observed in many different ways:

* "If the big, bad wolf goes down the chimney, he's going to get burned!" (Literacy)
* "If you give me one more cookie, I'll have two all together." (Math)
* "We forgot to water our plant and it died." (Science)
* "We have to wipe off the art tables so we can have snack tables." (Social Studies)
* "If you add too much water to the paint, it will run down the paper." (The Arts)

Children's cognitive development is more than memorizing facts. In the early childhood years, children are not only learning knowledge, skills, and concepts, but they are also acquiring the "learning to learn" skills that are so important for future learning.

Learning and Problem Solving

objective
22. Observes objects and events with curiosity

	I	II	III
Forerunners Looks at and touches object presented by an adult or another child Explores materials in the environment *e.g., touching, looking, smelling, mouthing, listening, playing*	Examines with attention to detail, noticing attributes of objects *e.g., points out stripes on caterpillar; notices it gets darker when the sun goes behind a cloud; points out changes in animals or plants in room*	Notices and/or asks questions about similarities and differences *e.g., points out that two trucks are the same size; asks why the leaves fall off the trees*	Observes attentively and seeks relevant information *e.g., describes key features of different models of cars (such as logos, number of doors, type of license plate); investigates which objects will sink and which will float*

15

Learning and Problem Solving, continued

objective
23. Approaches problems flexibly

	I	II	III
Forerunners Imitates adult or peer in solving problems Repeats and persists in trial and error approach	Finds multiple uses for classroom objects *e.g., uses wooden blocks as musical instruments; strings wooden beads into necklace for dress-up*	Experiments with materials in new ways when first way doesn't work *e.g., when playdough recipe produces sticky dough, asks for more flour; fills plastic bottle with water to make it sink*	Finds alternative solutions to problems *e.g., suggests using block as doorstop when classroom doorstop disappears; offers to swap trike for riding toy she wants and then adds firefighter hat to the bargain*

objective
24. Shows persistence in approaching tasks

	I	II	III
Forerunners Remains engaged in a task for short periods with assistance Stays involved in self-selected activity such as playing with playdough for short periods	Sees simple tasks through to completion *e.g., puts toys away before going on to next activity; completes 5-piece puzzle*	Continues to work on task even when encountering difficulties *e.g., rebuilds block tower when it tumbles; keeps trying different puzzle pieces when pieces aren't fitting together*	Works on task over time, leaving and returning to complete it *e.g., continues to work on Lego structure over 3-day period; creates grocery store out of hollow blocks, adding more detail each day, and involves other children in playing grocery*

objective
25. Explores cause and effect

	I	II	III
Forerunners Notices an effect *e.g., shows pleasure in turning light switch on and off, wants to do it again; repeatedly stacks blocks and watches them fall* Looks for something when it is out of sight	Notices and comments on effect *e.g., while shaking a jar of water says, "Look at the bubbles when I do this"; after spinning around and stopping says, "Spinning makes the room look like it's moving up and down"*	Wonders "what will happen if" and tests out possibilities *e.g., blows into cardboard tubes of different sizes to hear if different sounds are made; changes the incline of a board to make cars slide down faster*	Explains plans for testing cause and effect, and tries out ideas *e.g., places pennies one by one in 2 floating boats ("I'm seeing which boat sinks first"); mixes gray paint to match another batch ("Let's put in one drop of white at a time 'til it's right")*

16

Learning and Problem Solving, continued

objective
26. Applies knowledge or experience to a new context

	I	II	III
Forerunners Follows familiar self-help routines at school (toileting, eating)—may need assistance	Draws on everyday experiences and applies this knowledge to similar situations *e.g., washes hands after playing at sand table; rocks baby doll in arms*	Applies new information or vocabulary to an activity or interaction *e.g., comments, "We're bouncing like Tigger" when jumping up and down with peer; uses traffic-directing signals after seeing a police officer demonstrate them*	Generates a rule, strategy, or idea from one learning experience and applies it in a new context *e.g., after learning to access one computer program by clicking on icons, uses similar procedures to access others; suggests voting to resolve a classroom issue*

Logical Thinking

objective
27. Classifies objects

	I	II	III
Forerunners Finds two objects that are the same and comments or puts them together Groups similar kinds of toys together such as cars, blocks, or dolls	Sorts objects by one property such as size, shape, color, or use *e.g., sorts pebbles into three buckets by color; puts square block with other square blocks*	Sorts a group of objects by one property and then by another *e.g., collects leaves and sorts by size and then by color; puts self in group wearing shoes that tie and then in group with blue shoes*	Sorts objects into groups/subgroups and can state reason *e.g., sorts stickers into four piles ("Here are the stars that are silver and gold, and here are circles, silver and gold"); piles animals and then divides them into zoo and farm animals*

objective
28. Compares/measures

	I	II	III
Forerunners Notices something new or different *e.g., a new classmate or a new toy on the shelf* Notices similarities of objects *e.g., "We have the same shoes"*	Notices similarities and differences *e.g., states, "The rose is the only flower in our garden that smells"; "I can run fast in my new shoes"*	Uses comparative words related to number, size, shape, texture, weight, color, speed, volume *e.g., "This bucket is heavier than that one"; "Now the music is going faster"*	Understands/uses measurement words and some standard measurement tools *e.g., uses unit blocks to measure length of rug; "We need 2 cups of flour and 1 cup of salt to make dough"*

Logical Thinking, continued

objective
29. Arranges objects in a series

	I	II	III
Forerunners Uses self-correcting toys such as form boards and graduated stacking rings Sorts by one attribute *e.g., big blocks and little blocks*	Notices when one object in a series is out of place *e.g., removes the one measuring spoon out of place in a line and tries to put it in right place*	Figures out a logical order for a group of objects *e.g., makes necklace of graduated wooden beads; arranges magazine pictures of faces from nicest expression to meanest*	Through trial and error, arranges objects along a continuum according to two or more physical features *e.g., lines up bottle caps by height and width; sorts playdough cookies by size, color, and shape*

objective
30. Recognizes patterns and can repeat them

	I	II	III
Forerunners Completes a sentence that repeats in a familiar story Hums, sings, or responds to a chorus that repeats in a familiar song Completes a simple form board	Notices and recreates simple patterns with objects *e.g., makes a row of blocks alternating in size (big-small-big-small); strings beads in repeating patterns of 2 colors*	Extends patterns or creates simple patterns of own design *e.g., makes necklace of beads in which a sequence of 2 or more colors is repeated; continues block pattern of 2 colors*	Creates complex patterns of own design or by copying *e.g., imitates hand-clapping pattern (long clap followed by 3 short claps); designs a 3-color pattern using colored inch cubes and repeats it across the table*

objective
31. Shows awareness of time concepts and sequence

	I	II	III
Forerunners Follows steps in simple routine such as in dressing or at naptime Demonstrates understanding of what comes next in daily schedule *e.g., goes to the table anticipating mealtime*	Demonstrates understanding of the present and may refer to past and future *e.g., responds appropriately when asked, "What did you do this morning?"; talks about, "Later, when Mom comes to pick me up"*	Uses past and future tenses and time words appropriately *e.g., talks about tomorrow, yesterday, last week; says, "After work time, we go outside"*	Associates events with time-related concepts *e.g., "Tomorrow is Saturday so there's no school"; "My birthday was last week"; "I go to bed at night"*

Logical Thinking, continued

objective
32. Shows awareness of position in space

	I	II	III
Forerunners Moves objects from one container to another Follows simple positional directions with assistance *e.g., puts paper in trash can*	Shows comprehension of basic positional words and concepts *e.g., puts object* in, on, under, on top of, *or* next to *another object as requested*	Understands and uses positional words correctly *e.g., "Come sit near me"; "The fish food goes on the top shelf"*	Shows understanding that positional relationships vary with one's perspective *e.g., turns lotto card around so player opposite him can see it right side up; "I can reach the ring when I'm on the top step, but from here it's too far"*

objective
33. Uses one-to-one correspondence

	I	II	III
Forerunners Places an object in each designated space *e.g., puts a peg doll in each hole in a toy bus*	Matches pairs of objects in one-to-one correspondence *e.g., searches through dress-ups to find two shoes for her feet*	Places objects in one-to-one correspondence with another set *e.g., lines up brushes to make sure there is one for each jar of paint; goes around the table placing one cup at each child's place*	Uses one-to-one correspondence as a way to compare two sets *e.g., lines up cubes across from a friend's row to determine who has more; puts one rider next to each horse saying, "Are there enough horses for all the cowboys?"*

objective
34. Uses numbers and counting

	I	II	III
Forerunners Understands the concept of "one" *e.g., picks up one object when asked* Understands the concept of more *e.g., picks up more of something when directed, or asks for more cheese*	Imitates counting behavior using number names (may not always say one number per item or get the sequence right) *e.g., says the numbers from 1 to 5 while moving finger along a row of 8 items (not realizing that counting means one number per item)*	Counts correctly up to 5 or so using one number for each object (may not always keep track of what has or has not been counted) *e.g., counts out 5 pretzels taking one at a time from bowl; counts a collection of objects but may count an object more than one time*	Counts to 10 or so connecting number words and symbols to the objects counted and knows that the last number describes the total *e.g., counts 8 bottle caps and says, "I have 8"; spins dial, then moves board game piece 6 spaces; draws 5 figures to show members of family*

Representation and Symbolic Thinking

objective
35. Takes on pretend roles and situations

I | II | III

Forerunners	Performs and labels actions associated with a role	Offers a play theme and scenario	Engages in elaborate and sustained role play
Imitates simple action	*e.g., feeding the baby doll, says, "I'm the Mommy"; picks up phone and says, "Hello, is Suzie there?"*	*e.g., "Let's play school"; while listening to doll's heartbeat with stethoscope announces that it's time to get the baby to the hospital*	*e.g., suggests a play theme and discusses who will do what; discusses with peer what to buy at grocery store, takes pocketbook and goes to grocery store*
e.g., picks up phone; rocks baby			
With adult or peer support, imitates routines			
e.g., pretends to feed doll; pours coffee; pretends to sleep			

objective
36. Makes believe with objects

I | II | III

Forerunners	Interacts appropriately with real objects or replicas in pretend play	Uses substitute object or gesture to represent real object	Uses make-believe props in planned and sustained play
Imitates adult's or another child's use of familiar objects	*e.g., uses a broken phone to make a pretend phone call; puts playdough cookies on little plastic plates*	*e.g., holds hand to ear and pretends to dial phone; builds a sand castle and puts shell on top for "satellite dish"*	*e.g., pretends with a peer to be garage mechanics working on cars made of blocks; sets up scene for playing school—students sit on pillows and teacher has a box for a desk*
e.g., rocks doll; stirs the pot			
Interacts appropriately with objects with adult or peer support			
e.g., responds to pretend phone call by putting phone to ear and vocalizing			

objective
37. Makes and interprets representations

I | II | III

Forerunners	Draws or constructs and then names what it is	Draws or builds a construction that represents something specific	Plans then creates increasingly elaborate representations
Labels scribbles as people or common objects	*e.g., draws pictures with different shapes and says, "This is my house"; lines up unit blocks and says, "I'm making a road"*	*e.g., makes a helicopter with Bristle Blocks; draws 6 legs on insect after looking at beetle*	*e.g., uses blocks to make a maze for the class gerbil; draws fire truck and includes many details*
Interacts and builds with blocks			
Begins to use descriptive labels in construction play			
e.g., "house," "road"			

Language Development

A solid foundation in language development in the years before a child enters school will promote success in reading and writing in the future. Children who have rich language and literacy experiences in preschool are less likely to have difficulties learning to read later on.[3] We have organized objectives for language development under two goals.

Listening and Speaking

objective

38. Hears and discriminates the sounds of language

	I	II	III
Forerunners Notices sounds in the environment *e.g., pays attention to birds singing, sirens* Joins in nursery rhymes and songs	Plays with words, sounds, and rhymes *e.g., repeats songs, rhymes, and chants; says, "Oh you Silly Willy"*	Recognizes and invents rhymes and repetitive phrases; notices words that begin the same way *e.g., makes up silly rhymes ("Bo, Bo, Biddle, Bop"); says, "My name begins the same as popcorn and pig"*	Hears and repeats separate sounds in words; plays with sounds to create new words *e.g., claps hands 3 times when saying "Su-zan-na"; says, "Pass the bapkin [napkin]"*

objective

39. Expresses self using words and expanded sentences

	I	II	III
Forerunners Uses non-verbal gestures or single words to communicate *e.g., points to ball* Uses 2-word phrases *e.g., "All gone"; "Go out"*	Uses simple sentences (3-4 words) to express wants and needs *e.g., "I want the trike"*	Uses longer sentences (5-6 words) to communicate *e.g., "I want to ride the trike when we go outside"*	Uses more complex sentences to express ideas and feelings *e.g., "I hope we can go outside today because I want to ride the tricycle around the track"*

[3] National Research Council. *Preventing Reading Difficulties in Young Children.* Washington, DC: National Academy Press, 1998.

Listening and Speaking, continued

objective
40. Understands and follows oral directions

	I	II	III

Forerunners	Follows one-step directions	Follows two-step directions	Follows directions with more than two steps
Associates words with actions *e.g., says "throw" when sees ball thrown; throws when hears the word* Follows oral directions when combined with gestures *e.g., "come here" accompanied with gesture*	*e.g., "Please get a tissue"*	*e.g., "When you get inside, please hang up your coat"*	*e.g., follows directions to put clay in container, wipe table, and wash hands when activity is finished*

objective
41. Answers questions

	I	II	III

Forerunners	Answers simple questions with one or two words	Answers questions with a complete thought	Answers questions with details
Answers yes/no questions with words, gestures, or signs *e.g., points to purple paint when asked what color she wants*	*e.g., when asked for name says, "Curtis"; says, "Purple and blue" when asked the colors of paint*	*e.g., responds, "I took a bus to school"; "I want purple and blue paint"*	*e.g., describes a family trip when asked about weekend; says, "I want purple and blue like my new shoes so I can make lots of flowers"*

objective
42. Asks questions

	I	II	III

Forerunners	Asks simple questions	Asks questions to further understanding	Asks increasingly complex questions to further own understanding
Uses facial expressions/gestures to ask a question Uses rising intonation to ask questions *e.g., "Mama comes back?"* Uses some "wh" words (what and where) to ask questions *e.g., "What that?"*	*e.g., "What's for lunch?" "Can we play outside today?"*	*e.g., "Where did the snow go when it melted?" "Why does that man wear a uniform?"*	*e.g., "What happened to the water in the fish tank? Did the fish drink it?"*

Listening and Speaking, continued

objective
43. Actively participates in conversations

I	II	III

Forerunners	Responds to comments and questions from others	Responds to others' comments in a series of exchanges	Initiates and/or extends conversations for at least four exchanges
Initiates communication by smiling and/or eye contact			
Responds to social greetings	*e.g., when one child says, "I have new shoes," shows own shoes and says, "Look at my new shoes"*	*e.g., makes relevant comments during a group discussion; provides more information when message is not understood*	*e.g., while talking with a friend, asks questions about what happened, what friend did, and shares own ideas*
e.g., waves in response to "hello" or "bye-bye"			

Reading and Writing

objective
44. Enjoys and values reading

I	II	III

Forerunners	Listens to stories being read	Participates in story time interactively	Chooses to read on own; seeks information in books; sees self as reader
Looks at books and pictures with an adult or another child			
Chooses and looks at books independently	*e.g., asks teacher to read favorite story; repeats refrain when familiar book is read aloud*	*e.g., answers questions before, during, and after read-aloud session; relates story to self; acts out familiar story with puppets*	*e.g., gives reasons for liking a book; looks for other books by favorite author; uses book on birds to identify egg found on nature walk*
Completes phrases in familiar stories			

objective
45. Demonstrates understanding of print concepts

I	II	III

Forerunners	Knows that print carries the message	Shows general knowledge of how print works	Knows each spoken word can be written down and read
Points to print on page and says, "Read this"			
Recognizes logos	*e.g., points to printed label on shelf and says, "Cars go here"; looking at the name the teacher has written on another child's drawing, says, "Whose is this?"*	*e.g., runs finger over text left to right, top to bottom as he pretends to read; knows that names begin with a big letter*	*e.g., touches a written word for every spoken word in a story; looking at a menu asks, "Which word says pancakes?"*
e.g., McDonald's			
Recognizes book by cover			

Reading and Writing, continued

objective
46. Demonstrates knowledge of the alphabet

I — II — III

Forerunners	Recognizes and identifies a few letters by name	Recognizes and names many letters	Beginning to make letter-sound connections
Participates in songs and fingerplays about letters			
Points out print in environment	*e.g., points to a cereal box and says, "That's C like in my name"*	*e.g., uses alphabet stamps and names the letters—"D, T, M"*	*e.g., writes a big* M *and says, "This is for* Mommy*"*
e.g., name on cubby, exit sign			

objective
47. Uses emerging reading skills to make meaning from print

I — II — III

Forerunners	Uses illustrations to guess what the text says	Makes judgements about words and text by noticing features (other than letters or words)	Uses different strategies (known words, knowledge of letters and sounds, patterns in text) to make meaning from print
Uses familiar logos and words to read print			
e.g., cereal logos, "exit" and "stop" signs	*e.g., looking at* The Three Pigs, *says, "And the wolf blew down the pig's house"*	*e.g., "That must be Christopher's name because it's so long"; "You didn't write enough words. I said, 'A Book about the Dog Biff,' and you just wrote three words"*	*e.g., "That word says* book*"; anticipates what comes next based on pattern in* Brown Bear; *figures out which word says* banana *because he knows it starts with* b
Recognizes own name in print and uses it as a cue to find possessions			
e.g., cubby, cot, placemat			

objective
48. Comprehends and interprets meaning from books and other texts

I — II — III

Forerunners	Imitates act of reading in play	Compares and predicts story events; acts out main events of a familiar story	Retells a story including many details and draws connections between story events
Repeats words and actions demonstrated in books			
e.g., roars like a lion	*e.g., holds up book and pretends to read to baby doll; takes out phonebook in dramatic play area to make a phone call*	*e.g., compares own feelings about baby brother to those of character; re-enacts* Three Billy Goats Gruff	*e.g., says, "The wolf blew the house down because it wasn't strong"; uses flannel board to retell* The Very Hungry Caterpillar
Relates story to self and shares information			
e.g., after hearing a story about snow says, "I made a snowman"			

24

Reading and Writing, continued

objective
49. Understands the purpose of writing

	I	II	III

Forerunners	Imitates act of writing in play	Understands there is a way to write that conveys meaning	Writes to convey meaning
Watches when others write			
Pretends to write (scribble writes)	*e.g., pretends to write a prescription while playing clinic; scribble writes next to a picture*	*e.g., tells teacher, "Write this down so everyone can read it"; asks teacher, "How do I write Happy Birthday?"; says, "That's not writing, that's scribble-scrabble"*	*e.g., on drawing for sick friend, writes own name; copies teacher's sign, "Do Not Disturb," to put near block pattern; makes deliberate letter choices during writing ttempts*

objective
50. Writes letters and words

	I	II	III

Forerunners	Uses scribble writing and letter-like forms	Writes recognizable letters, especially those in own name	Uses letters that represent sounds in writing words
Scribbles with crayons			
Experiments with writing tools such as markers and pencils			
Draws simple pictures to represent something			

Taken together, the goals and objectives within these four areas of development, as shown on the Developmental Continuum, provide a well-marked path for observing children and noting their progress. (See Appendix B for a copy of the entire *Creative Curriculum* Developmental Continuum.) Armed with this knowledge, you will have a wealth of information to plan for each child and for implementing *The Creative Curriculum.* At the same time, you can address content in literacy, math, science, social studies, the arts, and technology, which are embedded in the *Curriculum* goals and objectives. In the next chapter we describe each of the content areas, show how they relate to our goals and objectives, and provide examples of how teaching and learning take place in a *Creative Curriculum* classroom.

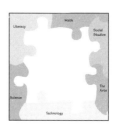

Chapter II
What Children Learn—
The Content of the Curriculum

Content standards for literacy, math, science, social studies, the arts, and technology provide both perspective and information to broaden and enrich your implementation of *The Creative Curriculum*. Perspective enables you to see where your teaching is leading children; information deepens your understanding of the subject area.

Every profession has a set of standards to guide it. The purpose of educational standards is to define what children should know and be able to do in a particular discipline. Standards give us a way of thinking about how big ideas develop over time. Because standards define what content is essential and worth knowing, they provide excellent guidance to curriculum developers and teachers.

It is not a simple task to base curriculum goals on standards and to use standards as a way of planning curriculum. Discussing standards can be a complex task for the following reasons:

❈ **There are multiple standards documents.** A number of national organizations representing different content areas have published standards. As states craft their own sets of content standards, they consult many different documents within each discipline.

❈ **There are varying definitions of standards.** Each discipline and each state has chosen to define standards in its own way. What may be considered a "standard" in one state might be called a "benchmark" or "desired results" in another.

❈ **They are organized by different grade levels.** National and state standards discuss what children should know and be able to do by certain grade levels. Some documents set "benchmarks" or checkpoints along the way at the fourth, eighth, and twelfth grades. Other documents, especially at the state and local level, define what children should know and be able to do at each grade level.

❈ **There are varying levels of specificity.** Some standards are written in very broad terms, others are quite specific.

In addition to the challenge of understanding these varying definitions, most national, state, and local standards documents are written for kindergarten through twelfth grade, and do not outline content for preschool children. However, we know that much learning that takes place during the preschool years paves the way to achieve these standards. The challenge for the early childhood profession is to think about these standards in a developmental way and consider how they relate to preschool.

To address these complex issues, we reviewed the significant documents in each subject area and identified key components useful to teachers of 3- to 5-year-old children. We considered what knowledge and skills were appropriate for this age group to develop. By identifying these key components, we hope to establish an important connection between the academic content areas and daily preschool experiences. As an example, let's look at the block area, see what children do, and how that relates to what children learn.

What Children Might Do and Say in the Block Area	What Content Areas Are Addressed
Build a road with blocks and note, "My road is eight blocks long. It's as long as this table."	Mathematics (number concepts, measurement)
Make a ramp and say, "Let's race our cars down the ramp."	Science (physical science)
Use markers and paper located in the block area to write a sign for their "building" that reads, 'Do nt nok dn.'	Literacy (print concepts)
Build a zoo with animals and a place for cars and buses to park after the teacher asks them, "Where do people park when they come to the zoo?"	Social Studies (geography)
Collect large, hollow blocks and ramps and explain, "We're building a bridge for the three Billy Goats Gruff."	The Arts (theater), Technology (technology tools), and Literacy (comprehension)

Once you become familiar with the content areas, you can plan rich experiences that offer a variety of opportunities for children to learn new skills and knowledge.

In the remaining sections of this chapter, we provide a description of the components of literacy, math, science, social studies, the arts, and technology. For each set of components, we illustrate how they relate to the goals and objectives in *The Creative Curriculum* and give examples of what you can do to help children develop and learn.

In Appendix D, we provide you with a tool that makes the link among the key components of the content areas, *The Creative Curriculum* goals and objectives, and standards documents that you may be responsible for implementing at the state or local level.

Literacy

Literacy is the growing ability to read and write. When parents of infants and toddlers talk to them and read them stories, a lifelong process of learning to read and write begins. Literacy skills—the ability to listen, speak, read, and write—develop interdependently in children. Several important reports address literacy development.

In 1996, the International Reading Association and the National Council of Teachers of English developed the *Standards for English Language Arts,*[4] which defined what children should know and be able to do in kindergarten through twelfth grade. However, this left little guidance about what should happen in the preschool years.

Two years later, the National Research Council published *Preventing Reading Difficulties in Young Children,*[5] which showed what language and literacy should look from birth through third grade. The Council later published *Starting Out Right: A Guide to Promoting Children's Reading Success*[6] to share its findings with teachers, parents, and child care providers.

In 1998, the International Reading Association (IRA) and the National Association for the Education of Young Children (NAEYC) jointly issued a position statement entitled, *Learning to Read and Write: Developmentally Appropriate Practices for Young Children.*[7] This statement provides teachers and policy makers with a set of principles and recommendations for children birth through age eight.

In 2000, the National Institute of Child Health and Human Development provided more guidance to the field.[8]

---

[4] International Reading Association and the National Council of Teachers of English. *Standards for the English Language Arts.* 1996.

[5] National Research Council. *Preventing Reading Difficulties in Young Children.* Washington, DC: National Academy Press, 1998.

[6] National Research Council. *Starting Out Right: A Guide to Promoting Children's Reading Success.* Washington, DC: National Academy Press, 1999.

[7] Neuman, Susan B., Carol Copple, and Sue Bredekamp. *Learning to Read and Write: Developmentally Appropriate Practices for Young Children.* Washington, DC: NAEYC, 2000.

[8] National Institute of Child Health and Human Development. *Report of the National Reading Panel: Teaching Children to Read: An Evidence-Based Assessment of the Scientific Research Literature on Reading and Its Implications for Reading Instruction.* (NIH Publication No. 00-4769). Washington, DC: U.S. Government Printing Office, 2000.

Key Components of Literacy

Using these documents, we describe seven key components of literacy for preschool children ages 3 to 5.

Objectives that focus on Increased Vocabulary and Language

3. Recognizes own feelings and manages them appropriately
38. Hears and discriminates the sounds of language
39. Expresses self using words and expanded sentences
40. Understands and follows oral directions
41. Answers questions
42. Asks questions
43. Actively participates in conversations

Increased Vocabulary and Language

When children are exposed to rich vocabulary through interesting conversations, they learn the words they will need to read and to write. Children who come from homes where parents talk to them a lot tend to have larger vocabularies and generally do better in school. Research tells us that children who have large vocabularies and understand spoken language have an easier time learning to read.[9] Talking to adults and to peers is a good way for children to learn new words and ideas.

In a *Creative Curriculum* classroom you hear lots of talking. Teachers use many opportunities to help children expand their vocabularies and develop their language skills. They do this through:

Informal conversations—When you have frequent one-on-one conversations with children, you provide opportunities for children to experience the two-way nature of conversations—e.g., you talk and I listen; I talk and you listen. Talk to children about their interests, what they do at home, or what they are playing. If a child is using incorrect grammar, respond by modeling it correctly. For example, if Joshua says, "Me go to the park last night," you might say, "Oh, I go to the park sometimes too. What did you do there?"

Songs, rhymes, fingerplays, or movement activities—Children learn many new words when they participate in music and movement activities throughout the day. When you begin the fingerplay, "These are grandmother's spectacles," and use your fingers to make circles over your eyes, children are learning a new word for glasses. As you sing "The Itsy Bitsy Spider," children can learn the meaning of the word *waterspout*.

Firsthand experiences—As children mold clay, sift sand, paint a picture, or pet a rabbit, you can help extend their vocabulary by using new words to describe what they are experiencing (e.g., sticky, smooth, soft).

---

9 Hart, B., and T. Risley. *Meaningful Differences in the Everyday Experience of Young Americans.* Baltimore: Paul H. Brookes, 1995, pp. 160-161.

Books—Books provide an excellent way of introducing children to new words. You might want to try one of these strategies:

❋ Preview the book with the children before you read it to them. Talk about some new words they may hear during the story.

❋ Point to the picture as you read to help children link the word to its meaning.

❋ After reading the entire book, go back to several pages and talk specifically about them.

❋ Relate the story to a real-life experience.

❋ Explain what the word means right after coming across it in the book.

❋ Read words, like *pop* or *fizz*, with expression so children can figure out the meaning.

What about children whose primary language is not English? Studies have shown that a strong basis in a first language promotes school achievement in a second language.[10] Children who are learning English as a second language are more likely to become readers and writers of English if they understand the vocabulary and concepts in their primary language first. The long-term goal is for children to be able to understand, speak, read, and write in their primary language and in English. Therefore, you want to support children's first language as you help them acquire oral proficiency in English.

Phonological Awareness

A key finding in recent research has been the importance of developing phonological awareness during the preschool years. It is common to confuse phonological awareness with phonics. They are not the same. *Phonological awareness* is the ability to attend to the different sounds of language, separate from their meaning. *Phonics,* on the other hand, is being able to connect a printed symbol with a sound. Phonological awareness comes first, so it's appropriate to help children develop this skill during the preschool years.

You can promote the development of phonological awareness by:

❋ introducing rhymes, poems, and rhyming songs;

❋ encouraging children to make up silly names for things by substituting one sound for another (e.g., "Silly Willy," "funny bunny");

> **Objectives that focus on
> Phonological Awareness**
>
> 38. Hears and discriminates the sounds of language
> 46. Demonstrates knowledge of the alphabet
> 50. Writes letters and words

---

10 *Preventing Reading Difficulties in Young Children*, pp. 236-237.

❊ breaking long words into syllables or clapping along with each syllable in a phrase (e.g., clapping twice while saying the name Kel-ly); and

❊ calling attention to how words sound—bag, bell, and box—all begin with the same sound.[11]

In preschool, the ability to hear and explore the sounds of language paves the way for a more advanced component of phonological awareness—phonemic awareness. A *phoneme* is the smallest unit of sound. For example, the word "cat" is made of three phonemes, /c/-/a/-/t/, and the word "chat" is also made of three phonemes, /ch/-/a/-/t/. *Phonemic awareness* is the knowledge that every spoken word is made up of a sequence of sounds that can be segmented and blended to form new words. The skills of segmenting and blending phonemes are important for phonics instruction and later reading, but they are typically more advanced expectations that are usually addressed at the end of kindergarten and during first grade. In preschool, however, you can draw children's attention to the sounds in words through playful activities such as songs, stories, and rhymes.

You can help children develop phonological awareness by:

❊ reading books that contain rhyme, rhythm, and repetition. One favorite is *Brown Bear* by Bill Martin, Jr. On repeated readings of a story, stop at the rhyming word and ask the children to complete the sentence ("Brown bear. Brown bear. What do you see? I see a red bird looking at ____.");

❊ reading books that play with words, such as Dr. Seuss books or *Silly Sally* by Audrey Wood;

❊ singing silly songs, such as "Willoughby, Wallaby, Woo" or "Bibbity, Bobbity, Boo," that draw attention to *alliteration* (a series of words all beginning with the same consonant sound or sound group);

❊ singing songs that help children learn more about rhyming words, such as "Down by the Bay"; and

❊ drawing children's attention to the sounds of words during daily activities. "If your name begins the same sound as these words—table, toes, turnips, tickle—you may go outside first."

A good foundation in phonological awareness in the preschool years is necessary so that later instruction in phonics and beginning reading can make sense.

---

[11] *Starting Out Right*, pp. 20-21.

Understanding Books and Other Texts

With a variety of books—narrative storybooks, predictable books (books with rhyme, repetition, and predictable language patterns), informational books, number books, alphabet books, poetry books—you can help children learn about the different forms of literature and the many pleasures to be found in books.

Reading good books to children every day helps them understand how a story works. They can learn that:

❀ stories have a beginning, middle, and end;
❀ there are different characters in a story;
❀ the story has a setting where it takes place;
❀ there is a sequence of events in a story; and
❀ a conversation might be taking place.

> Objectives that focus on **Understanding Books and Other Texts**
>
> 44. Enjoys and values reading
> 45. Demonstrates understanding of print concepts
> 47. Uses emerging reading skills to make meaning from print
> 48. Comprehends and interprets meaning from books and other texts
> 50. Writes letters and words

In preschool, children learn how to handle a book and begin to understand the purpose of books. They learn how to hold a book and can show you the front and back. As you read stories to children, you can expose them to words like *author* and *illustrator*. You can encourage children to become the authors of their own books.

But books are only one kind of text that can be read or written. We read and write signs, menus, letters, shopping lists, newspapers, invitations, messages, and journals. When you provide opportunities to use these different ways to communicate during their play, you help children discover the power and the purposes of reading and writing.

Knowledge of Print

Children who see print in the environment and use print in their play acquire an understanding of its importance. By drawing children's attention to the features of print during group times and play, you teach children important concepts about how print works. As children watch you write a story on a chart, you talk about how you are writing from left to right and from top to bottom. You may draw children's attention to the fact that names begin with a capital letter.

> Objectives that focus on **Knowledge of Print**
>
> 45. Demonstrates understanding of print concepts
> 46. Demonstrates knowledge of the alphabet
> 47. Uses emerging reading skills to make meaning from print
> 48. Comprehends and interprets meaning from books and other texts
> 49. Understands the purpose of writing
> 50. Writes letters and words

When you point out the sign that says *girls* or *boys* on the bathroom door, you help children learn that print conveys a message. When you read a note aloud that "Caroline will be going home with Kenya today," you demonstrate that the symbols on the paper are what is being read and that they mean something.

You can help children understand the functions of print. Place a "sign-up sheet" near a favorite activity such as the computer or the easel. Children "sign" their names if they would like to take a turn. At the beginning of the year, a child's signature may include only a few letter-like forms. As the year progresses, you will be able to notice recognizable letters.

Other ways to help children learn about the uses of print include: creating a message board for children to post notes they've written; posting a sign near the self-serve snack area that reads, "Take 3 cookies"; or encouraging children to write a letter to a sick friend.

Objectives that focus on **Letters and Words**

21. Uses tools for writing and drawing
37. Makes and interprets representations
46. Demonstrates knowledge of the alphabet
47. Uses emerging reading skills to make meaning from print
49. Understands the purpose of writing
50. Writes letters and words

Letters and Words

Learning about letters and words is an appropriate goal for preschool children. But what is most important is *how* this takes place. For starters, when you read big books, children see you turn pages of the book from front to back. They watch you sweep your hand under the text left-to-right and top-to-bottom. They also learn that what you are reading on the page are the words, not the pictures. As you write words or sentences on a chart, the children notice that you put a period or a question mark at the end of a sentence. They see you begin the first letter of their name or the first letter of a sentence with a capital letter and imitate that in their own writing. When you see a child leaving spaces between groups of letters you know he is developing a concept of "word."

Learning about letters is more than being able to recite the ABC song. When children really *know* about letters, they understand that a letter is a symbol representing one or more of the sounds in the English language; that these symbols can be grouped together to form words; and that these words have meaning. From our knowledge of child development, we know that children learn best what is meaningful and relevant to their own life experiences. When children learn their letters by rote or through flash cards and letter-of-the-week activities, the learning has little meaning. From a learner's point of view, it is hard to notice relationships among letters and see how letters are used in reading and writing when letters are taught in isolation. So how do you make learning about letters and words meaningful to young children?

The most important letter to children is the first letter of their names. Susan points to the "S" on a stop sign and says, "That's MY letter!" For this reason, helping children learn to recognize and read their names is a good starting point for learning about letters. Display children's names prominently in the classroom—on their cubbies, artwork, cots, and charts. Play lotto games or matching games with names and pictures. Talk about the alphabet when children play with cookie cutter letters in clay, magnetic letters, or alphabet blocks to help them understand more about letters.

Always include paper and writing tools in the interest areas so children can write letters and words that are meaningful to them during their play. They may want to dictate a message for you to write or write their own message for you to read. Often children like to refer to a model of the alphabet, so have the alphabet displayed at eye level or have it written on a card that can be picked up and handled. At times children may ask you how to spell a word that is important to them, such as *Mom*. There are a number of strategies you can use. You can say the word slowly. Or you may say, "It starts the same way as Marianne and Michael." Sometimes children just want the conventional spelling, so write it down for them to copy.

When a child writes "PG" above his drawing of a pig, you know that he has an understanding of beginning and ending sounds. Some people call this "invented spelling," "temporary spelling," "developmental spelling," or "phonetic spelling." Research has shown that invented spelling indicates that children are making sound-symbol connections. Recognize that it is a stage in spelling development and that other stages will follow. You can support and encourage children's attempts at writing by making comments such as, "Pig. That begins the same way as your name, Patrick."

Comprehension

The purpose of reading, writing, listening, and speaking is to communicate and understand meaning. Children who understand the meaning of stories and the meaning of the spoken words they hear in conversations are acquiring comprehension skills. They may ask questions or make comments relevant to the topic. They might relate a story to something that is familiar to them ("I went to the hospital once, just like Curious George."). There are other types of evidence of comprehension. A child may draw a picture about a story, retell the story on a flannel board, or act it out. Sometimes you might notice a child retelling a story to a stuffed animal or doll. You can encourage these types of activities by providing props, flannel board pieces, puppets, and magnetic boards that children can use to retell and act out familiar stories. All of these activities help children along the path to becoming competent and confident readers.

> Objectives that focus on
> **Comprehension**
>
> 44. Enjoys and values reading
> 45. Demonstrates understanding of print concepts
> 47. Uses emerging reading skills to make meaning from print
> 48. Comprehends and interprets meaning from books and other texts

To develop comprehension skills, *how* you read to children is very important. If you were reading *The Gingerbread Man* to your class, here are some comments and questions to help develop comprehension and critical thinking skills.

Kind of Question or Comment	Example
Completion—Leave off a word at the end of a sentence and let the children fill it in.	"Run, run, as fast as you can. You can't catch me. I'm the Gingerbread _____."
Open-ended—Ask the children a question that will make them think of several different answers.	"What do you think the Gingerbread Man is doing in this picture?"
Who, What, When, Where, Why, and How—Ask the children these kinds of questions about the story and the pictures.	"Who baked the Gingerbread Man?" "What did the little old man say when the Gingerbread Man ran away?" "Where did the fox want the Gingerbread Man to go?" "Why do you think the fox wanted the Gingerbread Man to ride on his head across the river?" "How did the fox trick the Gingerbread Man?"
Connections—Help the children see how the story relates to something familiar.	"Have any of you ever eaten gingerbread?"

When you use these prompts, they should be a natural part of your storybook reading. The first time you read a book, don't interrupt the flow of the story. Try not to ask more questions than the children can handle. Keep it light and keep it fun!

Literacy as a Source of Enjoyment

We know that people who read more tend to be better readers. They are motivated to read because they are excited about uncovering the plot of a story. Motivation is an important aspect of literacy.

To help the children in your class enjoy books, you can do the following:

> **Objectives that focus on Literacy as a Source of Enjoyment**
>
> 35. Takes on pretend roles and situations
> 38. Hears and discriminates the sounds of language
> 44. Enjoys and values reading
> 45. Demonstrates understanding of print concepts
> 47. Uses emerging reading skills to make meaning from print
> 48. Comprehends and interprets meaning from books and other texts

* Read to children in large groups, small groups, and one-on-one.
* Re-read favorite stories—children love hearing the same story over and over again.
* Read stories with expression—don't hold back, be dramatic!
* Listen to children as they make attempts to read.
* Create a warm, inviting library corner.
* Place books all around the room rather than just in the library corner (e.g., a book on castles in the block corner, a book about insects in the discovery area).
* Offer children literacy materials to enhance their play (e.g., writing tools, paper, magazines, books, envelopes).
* Let children see you reading and writing for pleasure or for a purpose.
* Encourage children to take books home to share with family members.

The role of the teacher is critical to literacy development. Teachers should thoughtfully and purposefully interact with children and plan experiences to support and extend literacy learning. Literacy does not just "happen," it is cultivated.

How the Components of Literacy Are Addressed in *The Creative Curriculum*®

COMPONENTS	*CREATIVE CURRICULUM* OBJECTIVES	WHAT TEACHERS DO
Increased Vocabulary and Language (Acquires new words and uses them to communicate)	3. Recognizes own feelings and manages them appropriately 38. Hears and discriminates the sounds of language 39. Expresses self using words and expanded sentences 40. Understands and follows oral directions 41. Answers questions 42. Asks questions 43. Actively participates in conversations	Engage in frequent one-on-one conversations with children. Provide children with many firsthand experiences and give them the words that describe what they are doing and learning. Introduce children to new words during storytime using various strategies (explaining; pointing to pictures; using expression, body language, or tone of voice). Lead children in singing songs and saying rhymes and fingerplays to learn new words.
Phonological Awareness (Hears and discriminates the sounds of spoken words; recognizes words that sound the same and words that sound different)	38. Hears and discriminates the sounds of language 46. Demonstrates knowledge of the alphabet 50. Writes letters and words	Sing songs, play language games, and say rhymes that encourage children to play with words. Talk about words and sounds during daily activities ("Karen, Kyle, and Kendra—your names all start the same way!") Read books that play with the sounds in words, such as Dr. Seuss books.
Understanding Books and Other Texts (Learns how to use a book and the purpose of books; gains a sense of story; learns about the uses of other texts such as signs, menus, magazines, newspapers, etc.)	44. Enjoys and values reading 45. Demonstrates understanding of print concepts 47. Uses emerging reading skills to make meaning from print 48. Comprehends and interprets meaning from books and other texts 50. Writes letters and words	Model how to handle books properly and teach children to care for them. Help children find books and magazines to learn more about topics that interest them. Add magazines, signs, pamphlets, telephone books, menus, and newspapers to dramatic play areas. Talk about the author and illustrator when introducing a story.

How the Components of Literacy Are Addressed in *The Creative Curriculum*®

COMPONENTS	*CREATIVE CURRICULUM* OBJECTIVES	WHAT TEACHERS DO
Knowledge of Print (Learns how print works)	45. Demonstrates understanding of print concepts 46. Demonstrates knowledge of the alphabet 47. Uses emerging reading skills to make meaning from print 48. Comprehends and interprets meaning from books and other texts 49. Understands the purpose of writing 50. Writes letters and words	Talk about features of print (top-to-bottom, left-to-right) while writing experience charts. Occasionally run your finger under the words as you read a story. As you write with children, draw their attention to symbols such as periods and question marks ("I better put a period here so others will know to stop when they are reading it").
Letters and Words (Identifies and writes some letters and words)	21. Uses tools for writing and drawing 37. Makes and interprets representations 46. Demonstrates knowledge of the alphabet 47. Uses emerging reading skills to make meaning from print 49. Understands the purpose of writing 50. Writes letters and words	Display the alphabet at children's eye level and have alphabet cards available for children to use during play. Add materials such as alphabet puzzles, magnetic letters, foam letters, paper, and pencils to the interest areas. Draw children's attention to letters and words in the environment as they use them in their everyday activities.
Comprehension (Understands and follows what is going on in a book, story, or conversation)	44. Enjoys and values reading 45. Demonstrates understanding of print concepts 47. Uses emerging reading skills to make meaning from print 48. Comprehends and interprets meaning from books and other texts	Add storytelling props to the library corner for retelling. Leave off a word at the end of a sentence when reading a predictable book. Ask children open-ended questions while reading ("What do you think will happen next?"). Encourage children to recall important events in a story ("Do you remember what happened when wolf blew on the house of straw?").
Literacy as a Source of Enjoyment (Enjoys being read to and reading and writing)	35. Takes on pretend roles and situations 38. Hears and discriminates the sounds of language 44. Enjoys and values reading 45. Demonstrates understanding of print concepts 47. Uses emerging reading skills to make meaning from print 48. Comprehends and interprets meaning from books and other texts	Arrange the library area attractively and include high-quality literature and soft, comfortable furniture. Read books to children and encourage them to talk about the story. Invite parents, grandparents, and special guests to read in the library area. Add interesting materials to the writing area to encourage writing attempts—pencils and pens, stationery, stamps, envelopes, etc.

Mathematics

Mathematics is the ability to think logically, to solve problems, and to notice relationships. It is one way to make sense of the world, because it helps us find order and logic by noticing patterns, making predictions, and solving problems.

Just as reading is not simply recognizing letters and sounds, mathematics is not simply recognizing numbers. When children are taught mathematics by rote memorization, they learn the facts but may be unable to apply what they have learned to problem-solving situations. As a result, they often become bored or intimidated by math.

The National Council of Teachers of Mathematics (NCTM) has developed a set of standards that guide the teaching of math in preschool through twelfth grade. The NCTM's *Principles and Standards for School Mathematics*[12] are divided into two groups. The five process standards focus on *how* children acquire and use mathematical knowledge—problem solving, reasoning, communication, connections, and representation. The five content standards address *what* math children should know—number concepts, patterns and relationships, geometry and spatial sense, measurement, and data analysis. You can address these standards by setting up an environment that invites mathematical thinking, planning purposeful mathematical experiences, and interacting with children during their play. The section below illustrates what these standards might look like in a preschool classroom. We have modified the titles of the standards slightly to make them more appropriate for preschoolers.

How Young Children Explore Mathematics (Process Skills)

To become mathematical thinkers, children need to explore, manipulate, and organize concrete materials before abstract symbols like written numbers can hold any meaning for them. Through play, children can begin to question, analyze, and discuss their discoveries and see how mathematics is part of everyday life. With direction and focus in their play, children can become logical thinkers and experience math as both useful and satisfying.

You can support children's mathematical thinking by planning additional experiences to help them develop particular mathematical ideas. When you have a good understanding of how math concepts develop over time, you can guide children to the next level of learning.

---

12 National Council of Teachers of Mathematics. *Principles and Standards for School Mathematics.* Reston, VA: NCTM, 2000.

Becoming Mathematical Problem Solvers

Young children between the ages of three and five are naturally engaged in mathematical problem solving. For example, a three-year-old will crawl into a small cardboard box looking for a cozy space. A four-year-old will study the blocks on the floor to see which one she needs to make the sides of a building the same height.

As children solve problems during their play, encourage them to share their thinking with you or with friends. How you interact with children can expand this ability. Creating an atmosphere in which children feel free to take risks will encourage them to continue trying to find solutions to problems. Asking open-ended questions or simply stating what you observe draws children's attention to their own problem-solving strategies:

* "I see that you divided the clay so each person has the same amount. How did you do that?"
* "You made a pattern around the edge of your picture—triangle, square, triangle, square."

Learning to Reason

Young children are naturally curious about the world around them. They often come up with reasons to explain why things happen. A child might say, for example, "The fish drank up all the water" to account for the falling water level in the aquarium. Developing the ability to reason helps children make sense of mathematics.

Obviously, preschoolers' reasoning may be full of misconceptions. A child might say that three cookies spread out on a plate are more than five that are arranged close together. Or a child may look at equal amounts of juice in two different containers, one short and the other tall, and say that the tall glass has more. Three- to five-year-old children tend to judge things by how they look. With many guided learning experiences, children refine their reasoning skills.

Children use reasoning skills when they sort, classify, pattern, and graph. They usually focus on one attribute at a time. For example, "I put these leaves together because they all have pointy edges."

The language you use as you interact with children will also help develop their reasoning abilities:

* "The reason we can't go out side today is *because* it is raining."
* "*If* you tear the pages in the book, *then* other children can't enjoy it."
* "You may have *either* a ball *or* a jump rope, *but not* both."

Learning to Make Connections

Children learn to make connections when they see how math relates to their own lives. When they put four candles on their birthday cake, set a table for five people, or close their eyes and count to ten while playing hide-and-seek, they are using math in a meaningful way.

Not only do preschoolers use math in every interest area of *The Creative Curriculum*, but they can also use math across the content areas.

- ❀ Literacy—learning about number relationships in stories such as *The Doorbell Rang* or *Five Little Monkeys*
- ❀ Science—making a graph of things that sink and float
- ❀ Social Studies—taking a walk in the neighborhood and counting fire hydrants
- ❀ The Arts—using rhythm instruments to tap a musical pattern
- ❀ Technology—ranking objects by size in a computer program

You can help children make connections by looking for opportunities to focus on math in everyday routines and activities. "Will you make sure that each paint pot has a brush?" or "It's time to come to group time when all of the sand has run through the sand timer" are examples of how you can make mathematical connections throughout the day.

Learning to Communicate Mathematically and Make Representations

To communicate mathematically, we have to know the language of mathematics. When children talk about and reflect on what they think and do in math, they gain a better understanding of what they are learning. Language—spoken, written, and visually represented—helps children clarify their thinking and structure their ideas.

You can design opportunities for children to communicate mathematically and represent their thinking in a number of ways:

- ❀ Graph objects found on a nature walk.
- ❀ Describe a pattern created with colored cubes.
- ❀ Draw a picture showing how many people are in the child's family.
- ❀ Make tally marks to describe the number of children who like bananas.
- ❀ Line up dolls from smallest to largest.
- ❀ Dramatize a story, song, or fingerplay that has mathematical relationships, such as *Ten in the Bed*.

For children who are not very verbal, or whose primary language is not English, communicating mathematical ideas in different ways gives them ways to demonstrate what they know and can do. For example, a child might create a pattern with colored blocks or extend a pattern that you have created. The child may not be able to explain what he did or to name the pattern, but he has demonstrated an understanding of the concept.

With these process goals in mind—becoming mathematical problem solvers, learning to reason, learning to make connections, and learning to communicate mathematically and make representations—you can prepare a learning environment in which children learn the content of math. How you interact with children to extend their thinking will influence how much they learn.

The Content of Mathematics in Preschool

Children need skills in specific areas to help them think mathematically. In preschool, the content of math includes:

* number concepts,
* patterns and relationships,
* geometry and spatial sense,
* measurement, and
* data collection, organization, and representation.

Number Concepts

> **Objectives that focus on Number Concepts**
>
> 22. Observes objects and events with curiosity
> 23. Approaches problems flexibly
> 28. Compares/measures
> 33. Uses one-to-one correspondence
> 34. Uses numbers and counting

Young children love to count! Once they develop this skill, they count everything—from the number of cookies on their plates to how many friends are joining in a game. Developing a sense of number concepts follows a developmental sequence.

Rote counting involves reciting the sequence of numbers by memory. Many children are able to recite numbers when they begin preschool. Singing number songs and saying number rhymes help to develop this ability. However, being able to recite numbers does not mean that a child understands what each number represents. Even though a child may be able to count to ten, she may not realize that ten is a symbol that represents a group of ten objects. When helping children learn to recognize number symbols, always relate them to a quantity.

One-to-one correspondence means matching a number word to an object in a group. A child who does not have this skill may say the number words faster or slower than he points to them. As this skill progresses, a child might count a set of ten objects correctly, but when given a larger set of objects, he might lose track. You can help children develop one-to-one correspondence by providing many opportunities to count things for a purpose. For example, how many napkins do we need to put on the table for snack time? When children are first learning to count a set of objects, encourage them to touch each object as they count.

When a child counts a set of objects, he needs to understand that the last number counted *includes* all of the objects that have been counted. If you ask a child to bring you three blocks and he only brings you the third block counted, then the idea of *inclusion* has not been developed. Children also figure out that no matter which order you counted the group of three blocks, the answer will still be the same—three. As children have more experience, they will be able to look at three crayons and tell you how many there are without counting.

Children love big numbers and are often fascinated by them. As they are ready to move on to counting past ten, provide children with experiences to nudge them gently to the next level of understanding. Use big numbers in your conversations with them, "There must be a thousand leaves in this pile" or "We have hundreds of Lego pieces in the bin."

Children develop number concepts when they have many opportunities to count for a purpose. They understand what "three" really means, and they begin to understand the relationships between quantities—e.g., more, less, and the same.

Objectives that focus on Patterns and Relationships

22. Observes objects and events with curiosity
23. Approaches problems flexibly
27. Classifies objects
28. Compares/measures
30. Recognizes patterns and can repeat them
37. Makes and interprets representations

Patterns and Relationships

Patterns and relationships refer to any kind of sequence, repetition, organization, or cause and effect. Pattern recognition develops important problem-solving skills. To identify, extend, and create patterns, a child must be able to organize information, perceive similarities and differences, and make judgments.

Young children benefit from opportunities to play with patterns and notice relationships using all their senses: seeing, hearing, touching, and even tasting and smelling. For example, you can help children notice patterns in the repeating lines on a sidewalk, the veins on leaves, the sounds of a foghorn at the harbor, the texture of the bricks on the school building, and the smells coming from the cafeteria at the same time each day. Children become aware of patterns when they are encouraged to "read" their patterns aloud.

After children learn to recognize repeating patterns, you can encourage them to copy patterns and extend them. While at the table toy area, you may play a game where you create a pattern using colored cubes (red, blue, red, blue), and the child copies your pattern. You can also lead children in clapping rhythmical patterns. As you play music, alternate clapping your hands and patting your thighs and encourage the children to follow. Create more complicated patterns later such as *clap, clap, pat...clap, clap, pat.*

Eventually, children are able to create their own patterns. They may make a patterned border around a picture or create a patterned wall in a block structure. Support their learning by helping them name the patterns they have created.

Geometry and Spatial Sense

When children explore the shapes and structures in their environment, they begin to think about concepts of space and learn about geometry. They explore two- and three-dimensional shapes during their everyday experiences in the classroom. Creating designs with pattern blocks; drawing, painting, and cutting shapes in their artwork; and returning blocks on the shelves by sorting them are all ways that children begin to under-stand about geometric shapes. Take children on a walk in the neighborhood and help them locate shapes in the environment. Describe the shapes that you see children create: "I see you made a triangle with three strips of paper."

Children gain spatial sense as they maneuver through an obstacle course and hear the words—*over, under, through, beside, below.* In the block corner, they hear another child say to put the horse *inside* the fence or put the block *on top of* the building. Use these spatial terms during everyday activities. Play games or prompt children during movement activities to help them gain spatial sense. For example, have children run *under* the parachute or wave the scarf *over* their heads.

Helping children develop geometry and spatial sense leads the way to understanding other topics in math, science, social studies, the arts, and technology.

Objectives that focus on Geometry and Spatial Sense

22. Observes objects and events with curiosity
23. Approaches problems flexibly
27. Classifies objects
28. Compares/measures
32. Shows awareness of position in space
37. Makes and interprets representations

Measurement

Measurement is a mathematical skill we use every day. The focus of measurement activities in preschool is on developing an understanding of the principles and uses of measuring, rather than on specific skills. Children benefit from opportunities to use materials and partici-pate in hands-on activities that help them increase their understanding of the concept of measurement.

Objectives that focus on Measurement

22. Observes objects and events with curiosity
23. Approaches problems flexibly
27. Classifies objects
28. Compares/measures
29. Arranges objects in a series
31. Shows awareness of time concepts and sequence
34. Uses numbers and counting

Introduce materials, such as clocks, scales, thermometers, measuring cups, and rulers, and make them available for children's explorations. Children can make their own measuring tools. For example, they can trace and cut out paper hands and feet to use for measuring length or area. Your guidance and encouragement to describe their thinking and actions help children better understand these experiences.

Objectives that focus on Data Collection, Organization, and Representation

22. Observes objects and events with curiosity
23. Approaches problems flexibly
27. Classifies objects
28. Compares/measures
29. Arranges objects in a series
30. Recognizes patterns and can repeat them
33. Uses one-to-one correspondence
34. Uses numbers and counting
37. Makes and interprets representations

Data Collection, Organization, and Representation

Young children ask many questions about the world around them. When they learn how to find answers to their questions, organize the information, and draw some conclusions, they can use this skill throughout life as an approach to learning. To answer their questions children sort, classify, graph, count, measure, and compare.

Sorting and classifying are essential beginning math activities that promote the development of logical thinking skills. The need for these skills arises naturally in preschool children. At this age, children love to make and use collections. They may begin to sort and make sets without any plan in mind. Then they begin to sort more purposely—for example, by properties such as color, shape, or size. As children develop and refine their sorting skills, they can sort by more than one attribute. By encouraging them to describe their sorting rules, you extend their mathematical thinking. Questions and statements such as, "How did you make your group?" or "Tell me how these are alike" or "Where would this one go?" help children verbalize their thinking and provide teachers with an assessment of what children know.

Graphing is a direct extension of sorting and classifying. A graph presents information in a visually organized way that helps children see relationships. Graphing is a way for children to display many different kinds of information in different forms. A simple graph of the kinds of shoes children are wearing could develop from a concrete representation to a symbolic one.

❋ *Concrete*—shoes with ties, Velcro, or buckles and slip-on shoes
❋ *Symbolic*—pictures representing the types of shoes

After children have learned how to display data in graph form, they can analyze and interpret the data. This involves comparing, counting, adding and subtracting, and using terms such as greater than, less than, equal, and not equal. The graph on the next page was made after the children in one classroom collected leaves on a walk.

To help children interpret this graph, a teacher might ask questions such as:

❈ "Which kind of leaf did we collect the most of? The least?"
❈ "Which leaves did we collect the same number of?"
❈ "What else does this graph tell us?"

How the Components of Math Are Addressed in *The Creative Curriculum®*

COMPONENTS	*CREATIVE CURRICULUM* OBJECTIVES	WHAT TEACHERS DO
Number Concepts (Understands numbers, ways of representing numbers, and relationships between numbers)	22. Observes objects and events with curiosity 23. Approaches problems flexibly 28. Compares/measures 33. Uses one-to-one correspondence 34. Uses numbers and counting	Teach children counting songs, rhymes, and chants (e.g., "1, 2, 3, 4, 5, I caught a fish alive"). Count during daily activities—the children present, the cups needed for each child, the paintbrushes needed for each container. Compare relationships between quantities ("There are more boys here today than girls.").
Patterns and Relationships (Recognizes, copies, extends patterns; makes predictions about patterns in the environment)	22. Observes objects and events with curiosity 23. Approaches problems flexibly 27. Classifies objects 28. Compares/measures 30. Recognizes patterns and can repeat them 37. Makes and interprets representations	Clap hands then pat thighs in a pattern (clap, pat, clap, pat). Later move to more complex patterns (clap, clap, pat, clap, clap, pat). Create "people patterns" with children (stand, sit, stand, sit) and help them describe the pattern. Draw children's attention to various patterns in the environment ("I see a pattern in your shirt today—red, blue, red, blue."). Describe patterns you see children creating ("You made a pattern with the blocks—square, triangle, square, triangle").
Geometry and Spatial Sense (Recognizes, names, builds, draws, describes, compares and sorts two- and three-dimensional shapes; recognizes and describes spatial relationships)	22. Observes objects and events with curiosity 23. Approaches problems flexibly 27. Classifies objects 28. Compares/measures 32. Shows awareness of position in space 37. Makes and interprets representations	Talk about the geometric shapes as children use blocks or shape blocks. Provide empty boxes, tubes, and containers for children to use in creating and constructing. Take children on a walk looking for shapes in the environment. Describe spatial relationships you notice as children play ("You're putting the horse inside the fence you made").

48

How the Components of Math Are Addressed in *The Creative Curriculum*®

COMPONENTS	*CREATIVE CURRICULUM* OBJECTIVES	WHAT TEACHERS DO
Measurement (Uses non-standard units to measure and make comparisons)	22. Observes objects and events with curiosity 23. Approaches problems flexibly 27. Classifies objects 28. Compares/measures 29. Arranges objects in a series 31. Shows awareness of time concepts and sequence 34. Uses numbers and counting	Show children how to use objects to measure things ("Look. This table is 5 blocks long"). Use a sand timer or kitchen timer to let children know that there are only 5 minutes left until clean-up time. Ask open-ended questions during measurement activities ("I wonder how many cups of water your pitcher will hold"). Use words like before, after, next, yesterday, today, tomorrow throughout the day ("Tomorrow is Mia's birthday").
Data Collection, Organization, and Representation (Poses questions to investigate, organizes responses, and creates representations of data)	22. Observes objects and events with curiosity 23. Approaches problems flexibly 27. Classifies objects 28. Compares/measures 29. Arranges objects in a series 30. Recognizes patterns and can repeat them 33. Uses one-to-one correspondence 34. Uses numbers and counting 37. Makes and interprets representations	Pose a "question of the day." Show children how to make tally marks under "yes" or "no" on a clipboard ("Do you like chocolate ice cream?"). Graph collections of objects found in the classroom such as stickers, leaves, rocks, shells, buttons, etc. Have the children form a "people graph" in response to your questions ("Are there more children here with brown hair than blonde hair?").

Science

In too many early childhood classrooms, science consists of a table filled with collections of leaves, shells, acorns, and other natural materials. These collections remain on the table for a while, and then the children tend to ignore them. While collections can be very interesting, simply displaying them does not promote scientific thinking. Science is an active process of inquiry and investigation, not a static table of collections. It is a way of thinking and acting, asking questions, and solving problems.

The *National Science Education Standards*[13] help teachers understand that science is more than memorizing facts. Science is a combination of both process skills (how they learn) and content (what they learn).

---

[13] National Research Council. *National Science Education Standards*. Washington, DC: National Academy Press, 1998.

How Young Children Explore Science (Process Skills)

Young children are natural scientists; they are curious, full of wonder, and eager to investigate. Young children do the work of scientists as part of their everyday lives—for example, when they observe their surroundings, test things out, and make discoveries. Squeezing a banana, examining an earthworm, and pouring sand through a sieve are a few ways in which young children experiment with and observe the material world. Using all their senses—touch, sight, smell, taste, and hearing—they discover relationships of change and growth and cause and effect. This is scientific thinking.

These process skills are also known as *inquiry* skills. As children learn about how plants grow, what makes a shadow, or why ice melts, they use these process skills to make predictions, test their ideas, and observe their outcomes.

Asking Scientific Questions

You can build on children's natural curiosity by showing them that their questions are worthwhile and helping them to see how their questions can become the basis for an investigation. By wondering aloud as you work with children, you help them pose scientific questions:

* "What do you think would happen if. . .?"
* "How do you think we will find out. . .?"
* "What do you see happening when. . .?"
* "Why do you think that happened?"
* "How would you describe what you see?"

Planning and Conducting Investigations

Young children generate explanations and new ideas all the time. The more experience they have with scientific investigations, the more accurate their ideas become. Observing what is happening in and around the classroom and creating a sense of wonder will lead to investigations that are meaningful to children. For example, suppose a child asks, "Why did our plant die?" Rather than giving the answer immediately, ask the children for possible reasons. Some may think it didn't get enough water, while others may think it needed more sunlight or plant food, or maybe it was just old. To find answers to the question, you might try to grow plants in the sun and in the shade to see which ones do better. Or you might try to grow one with plant food and one with none.

Other situations that are perfect for scientific investigations may emerge during daily routines or as children play in various interest areas.

During clean-up time—As children prepare to wipe up finger paints from the table, you might ask: "Tenesha, what do you think might happen if you used a wet sponge to wipe up the paint and I used a dry sponge? Shall we try?" Then you might ask, "What do you notice? Why do you think that happens?"

At the sand table—As children play, you might ask: "Which kind of sand do you think can make a bigger pile, wet or dry? Would you like to experiment?" And then, "What did you find out? Why do you think that happened?"

In the block corner—As you observe children building, you might ask: "Which wall is the strongest? Why do you think so?" And then, "How could you test the walls? What did you find out?"

Another way to bring science into the classroom is to set up investigations that will lead to discoveries. For example, set up containers of colored water, eyedroppers, and wax paper. Show children how to combine drops of water to create new colors.

Gathering Data

One of the most important ways that scientists collect data is through observation. Like scientists, children use their senses to learn about the world around them. Learning to observe means relying on all the senses and being able to choose and use tools for observation, such as a magnifying glass or a balance scale.

You can help children develop their observation skills by encouraging them to use all their senses:

Look—Talk about the size, color, shape, and position of objects; count features.
Touch—Talk about whether objects feel rough, smooth, wet, dry, oily, scaly, heavy, light, bumpy.
Listen—Notice the loudness or softness of sounds and compare sounds such as falling rain or a crashing toy.
Smell—Describe how something smells and compare new smells to familiar ones ("It smells like lemons" or "It smells like flowers").
Taste—Use words like sweet, bitter, sour, or spicy when tasting foods.

When you help children become careful observers who can describe what they see, you promote their confidence and competence as scientific thinkers.

Constructing Explanations and Communicating Findings

As children gather information, you can encourage them to classify by similarities and differences and to describe what they see through drawings, graphs, and discussions. And just as scientists share and discuss their discoveries in many ways, children can, too. They can talk about what they have seen or done, draw pictures and diagrams, make constructions or designs, dictate findings to you or a tape recorder, and keep written records.

The Content of Science in Preschool

In addition to the science inquiry skills, preschoolers can begin to acquire a foundation of science concepts and knowledge on which they can build. We know that young children learn best by using their senses to explore the world around them—that is, their immediate surroundings. To decide on *what* concepts children should learn in science, the best place to start is with what children see and do every day. Science concepts that emerge from children's everyday experiences will fit into one of these categories:

* Physical Science
* Life Science
* Earth and the Environment

Objectives that focus on Physical Science

22. Observes objects and events with curiosity
25. Explores cause and effect
27. Classifies objects
28. Compares/measures
29. Arranges objects in a series
30. Recognizes patterns and can repeat them
32. Shows awareness of position in space

Physical Science

When children make a block ramp to race cars, look through a kaleidoscope, or pick up objects with magnets, they are learning about the physical properties of objects. Opportunities to learn about physical science can be found throughout *The Creative Curriculum* classroom:

* **Blocks**—balancing, moving toy cars, weighing blocks
* **Dramatic play**—using kitchen tools such as an eggbeater, sand timer
* **Sand and water**—experimenting with water wheels, funnels, sifters
* **Table toys**—using magnetic letters, sorting texture cards, or smelling jars
* **Art and woodworking**—mixing paint colors or clay, using woodworking tools
* **Outdoors**—using playground equipment, playing with balls, digging in dirt

While interacting with children, you can talk about how things work. Ask open-ended questions that will encourage children to investigate more:

"I wonder what would happen if you tilted the ramp more before rolling the car down?" Set up a take-apart table so that children can find out how the gears work in an old clock or how a flashlight turns on and off. As you consider children's interests, think about some possible topics for investigation such as magnets, objects that sink and float, how things move, hot and cold, and how things work.

Life Science

Preschoolers are eager to learn about the living things around them. Caring for plants and animals in a preschool classroom helps children understand scientific concepts. They learn that most living things need food, water, and air to live. They begin to understand the difference between living and non-living things. As children learn about their bodies and how to stay healthy, they also learn about life science.

Children will learn these "big ideas" of the life sciences as they explore living things in their immediate environment. For example, by having a classroom pet, children learn how and what it eats, how it moves, how it sleeps, and how it cares for its young. Observing firsthand is far superior to teaching a child to identify a picture of an unfamiliar animal. Similarly, planting flowers, fruits, or vegetables gives children firsthand knowledge of what is takes to grow things Thus, topics preschoolers might focus on include real animals and plants or their own bodies and how they grow.

> **Objectives that focus on Life Science**
>
> 7. Respects and cares for classroom environment and materials
> 12. Shares and respects the rights of others
> 22. Observes objects and events with curiosity
> 25. Explores cause and effect
> 31. Shows awareness of time concepts and sequence

Earth and the Environment

Children learn about the environment when they do firsthand research. Learning about the planets or the fact that the earth rotates on its axis is not information preschoolers can investigate through their own explorations. Exploring shadows, however, is something they can investigate firsthand. Children can learn about the earth as they talk about the weather, explore rocks, or use recycled materials in the art center.

Explore the properties of the earth by asking children to bring in a cup of dirt from their yard at home. Children can sift the dirt and make comparisons of color and texture.

By thinking about what materials and experiences are available to children, you can consider studying topics such as day and night, shadows, weather, earth surfaces (rock, dirt, water, grass), recycling, and caring for the environment.

> **Objectives that focus on Earth and the Environment**
>
> 7. Respects and cares for classroom environment and materials
> 25. Explores cause and effect
> 27. Classifies objects
> 28. Compares/measures
> 31. Shows awareness of time concepts and sequence
> 32. Shows awareness of position in space

How the Components of Science Are Addressed in *The Creative Curriculum®*

COMPONENTS	CREATIVE CURRICULUM OBJECTIVES	WHAT TEACHERS DO
Physical Science (Explores the physical properties of the world by observing and manipulating common objects and materials in the environment)	22. Observes objects and events with curiosity 25. Explores cause and effect 27. Classifies objects 28. Compares/measures 29. Arranges objects in a series 30. Recognizes patterns and can repeat them 32. Shows awareness of position in space	Include science materials such as magnets, magnifying glasses, balance scales, pulleys, mirrors to encourage exploration. Use open-ended questions to further investigations ("I wonder why this big toy boat floats but the penny sinks"). Describe physical changes you see taking place ("When your blue paint ran into the yellow paint, it turned green!"). Include old small appliances or broken toys on a "take-apart" table to help children learn how things work.
Life Science (Explores living things, their life cycles, and their habitats)	7. Respects and cares for classroom environment and materials 12. Shares and respects the rights of others 22. Observes objects and events with curiosity 25. Explores cause and effect 31. Shows awareness of time concepts and sequence	Add living things such as plants and pets to the classroom and study them. After planting seeds with the children, provide markers and paper so they can observe and record the growth over time. During a study of houses, talk with children about animal homes such as bird's nests, beehives, anthills, etc. Observe and discuss life cycles of animals such as butterflies and frogs. Help children learn about health and their bodies every day ("Can you feel your heart pounding after running so much?" "Those carrots are so good for you").
Earth and the Environment (Explores the properties of the world around them, notices changes, and makes predictions)	7. Respects and cares for classroom environment and materials 25. Explores cause and effect 27. Classifies objects 28. Compares/measures 31. Shows awareness of time concepts and sequence 32. Shows awareness of position in space	Lead a discussion about things we do during the day and things we do at night. Paint with water on the sidewalk and talk about why it disappears. Play shadow tag and measure shadows. Talk about the seasons as you notice the changes in your environment ("I can tell fall is here. The leaves are turning red, yellow, orange, and brown"). Discuss the weather each day ("Jeremy, will you check the weather outside today? Do we need to wear sweaters?").

Social Studies

Social studies is the study of people—how people live today and lived in the past, how they work, get along with others, solve problems, shape, and are shaped by their surroundings. Learning in social studies begins at birth as infants develop relationships with significant adults, learn to communicate, and explore the world around them. In preschool, children continue this learning, extending it to their families and the people in their communities. In the process, they form understandings that relate to geography, civics, and history.

National standards have been written for several of the various fields of social studies—history, geography, economics, civics—and some states have also developed their own standards. In this section, we identify the big ideas of the various social studies standards documents and make them relevant for preschool.

How Preschool Children Explore Social Studies

The skills children acquire as they investigate topics in social studies teach them how to be researchers: to ask questions, to seek information, and to think about what they discover. Researchers go through a process using the following skills:

* ask a question or identify a problem,
* gather information,
* analyze information, and
* draw conclusions.

Ask a Question or Identify a Problem

In a classroom filled with interesting things to explore, there are many questions to ask and many problems to solve. In addition, using the surrounding community as your "textbook" for learning about the world provides innumerable opportunities for children to be inquisitive.

* "Where does the garbage truck take the trash?"
* "If they cut down the tree on the playground, where will we go when it's hot?"
* "There are so many people at the sand table that I can't play."

How you respond to children's questions and how you discuss problems are important in developing thinking skills in social studies. These questions reflect children's thinking and can lead to more in-depth studies.

Gather Information

After a question has been asked or a problem identified, information must be gathered. Preschool children gather information as they make observations, go on a field trip, look at books, or talk to experts. Children use all of their senses to gather information about the world around them.

* Mark sees a bulldozer and looks for a picture of one in a book about trucks.
* The children observe a delivery truck bringing food to the cafeteria.
* A fireman tells how his coat protects him from fire.

Analyze Information

Once children have gathered information, they might notice similarities and differences and sort, classify, and graph to analyze the information. At group time, you might lead a discussion about what you have observed. Because social studies includes the study of people and cultures, there may be many questions that have no single answer.

* Jamie sorts photographs of classmates by hair color.
* Tony makes a graph of the different kinds of homes each child lives in (e.g., apartment, trailer, one-story house).

Draw Conclusions

After getting information from many sources, sharing their own views, and hearing others, children can begin to make sense of what they have learned. With many experiences in the world around them, they can draw some conclusions.

* "You're not in my family because you don't live in my house."
* "If we sell cookies we can get money to fix our broken tricycle."

The kinds of questions you ask or the statements you make can lead children to draw conclusions.

The Content of Social Studies in Preschool

Children begin at infancy learning about **geography**—exploring physical space by crawling, climbing, digging, and splashing. When preschoolers maneuver a piece around a board game like Candyland, figure out how to ride around a tricycle path, or draw a treasure map, they are using beginning mapping skills. Preschoolers learn about **civics** as they begin to cooperate to resolve differences in a classroom setting. Learning about **history** is a bit more subtle, because history tells the story of changes that take place in the past. To a preschooler the past may be what happened this morning or yesterday. This being the case, you teach history each time you talk about the everyday events and routines that have happened in the classroom. Children learn about time from the daily, predictable routines you establish—a story before rest time, circle time after interest areas, and outdoor play after lunch. **Economics** includes the study of how goods and services are produced and distributed. When you set up a play grocery store, and help children learn about jobs and buying and selling, you are helping them learn about economics. Economics learning continues as preschoolers visit the supermarket, the doctor, the hardware store, the shoe store, and the playground.

Children in preschool learn about social studies firsthand. As members of a classroom community they have opportunities to live, work, and share with others. In such an environment, children learn the rudiments of living in a democratic society.

Spatial or Geographic Thinking

Geographic thinking begins with understanding space, becoming aware of the characteristics of the place where you live, and thinking about that place's location in relation to other places. In preschool, children can study the physical characteristics of their world—the sandbox area, the slides, the swings, and the grassy area by the tree—and talk about how to navigate in it. They can talk about mapping by discussing directions—how to get to the bathroom, the playground, the carpool line. They can recreate their neighborhood in the block area and draw or paint maps of places they go. An important goal is for children to begin to understand that maps represent actual places.

> Objectives that focus on
> **Spatial or Geographic Thinking**
>
> 22. Observes objects and events with curiosity
> 23. Approaches problems flexibly
> 25. Explores cause and effect
> 32. Shows awareness of position in space
> 37. Makes and interprets representations

You can help children learn more about spatial or geographic thinking by:

* providing concrete, direct experiences with their immediate environment;
* helping them distinguish between living and non-living things;
* talking about and exploring different surfaces on the earth—dirt, grass, sand, rocks;
* introducing games and movement activities to learn directional terms; and
* encouraging children to draw maps or build maps with blocks.

People and How They Live

Learning about people means recognizing physical characteristics; noticing similarities and differences in habits, homes, and work; thinking about family structures and roles; and recognizing how people rely on each other for goods and services. Preschool children can begin to explore these ideas by studying themselves and their families and thinking about rules in the classroom and how they help people live together and get along.

To help children learn more about people and how they live you can:

* talk about ways that all people are alike;
* invite families to participate in classroom activities;
* create graphs showing the number of people in children's families;
* display photographs of family members and encourage children to talk about them;
* visit businesses in the community and talk about the jobs various people do;
* set up dramatic play areas of familiar stores or occupations—grocery store, doctor's office, fast food restaurant; or
* develop classroom rules with children as needed.

People and the Environment

People affect the environment by changing it—building cities, making roads, building a highway or dam—and by protecting it—cleaning up a park, recycling, saving some green space from development. In preschool, children can explore the area near their homes or school to learn more about the local environment.

You can help children learn more about how people affect the environment by:

* recycling materials in the classroom;
* using recycled materials in the art area;
* talking about changes that take place in the environment around you (a fire destroying the woods, fish dying because of pollution, trees being cut down to make way for a road or a parking lot); or
* planting a tree on the playground.

People and the Past

While an adult understanding of chronological time is essential to understanding history, preschool children are focused on the *here* and *now*. They can begin to learn about time in relation to themselves. They can talk about their daily schedule, what they did yesterday, and what they will do tomorrow. Preschool children love to consider what they can do now that they couldn't do when they were "babies." They can appreciate stories about other times and places if the topics are relevant to their own experiences.

To further children's understanding about the past, you can:

* use words that explain the passage of time (yesterday, tomorrow, today, next week);
* ask children questions that will help them recall the past ("What did you do yesterday when you got home?");
* invite grandparents in to share stories about their childhood;
* compare children's baby clothes to the clothes they are wearing now; or
* compare tools used long ago with tools used today (a hand eggbeater and an electric beater).

Objectives that focus on
People and the Past

22. Observes objects and events with curiosity
25. Explores cause and effect
29. Arranges objects in a series
31. Shows awareness of time concepts and sequence
35. Takes on pretend roles and situations

How the Components of Social Studies Are Addressed in *The Creative Curriculum*®

COMPONENTS	CREATIVE CURRICULUM OBJECTIVES	WHAT TEACHERS DO
Spatial or Geographic Thinking (Learns about the physical world around us and how we move about the world)	22. Observes objects and events with curiosity 23. Approaches problems flexibly 25. Explores cause and effect 32. Shows awareness of position in space 37. Makes and interprets representations	Provide board games like Candyland as a way of introducing beginning mapping skills. Create an obstacle course for children to maneuver in, around, and through. Mark the shadow of a tree or a flagpole at different times of the day and talk about reasons why it changed. Draw children's attention to the physical properties of the earth as they dig in the dirt and create mud by adding water ("There are lots of small rocks in the dirt you're digging. Would you like a sifter?").
People and How They Live (Recognizes and respects likenesses and differences in people; recognizes how people rely on each other for goods and services; learns social skills; understands the need for rules)	1. Shows ability to adjust to new situations 3. Recognizes own feelings and manages them appropriately 4. Stands up for rights 9. Follows classroom rules 10. Plays well with other children 11. Recognizes the feelings of others and responds appropriately 12. Shares and respects the rights of others 13. Uses thinking skills to resolve conflicts	Create classroom rules with the children as the need arises ("There was a problem at the sand table today. Is there a rule we could make so everyone has enough room to play?"). Provide paint, crayons, markers, and construction paper in various skin tones. Taste foods from different cultures. Use the words of the various cultures represented in your class. Introduce new props to the dramatic play area that focus on jobs—flower shop, auto repair, restaurants, grocery store. Visit different stores in your neighborhood and discuss the jobs people do. Provide materials to create sculptures made from junk.
People and the Environment (Learns how people affect the environment by changing it and protecting it)	7. Respects and cares for classroom environment and materials 22. Observes objects and events with curiosity 23. Approaches problems flexibly 25. Explores cause and effect	Plant trees in the schoolyard. Encourage children to place trash in wastebasket in the classroom and on the playground. Recycle cardboard tubes and boxes and use in the block corner or art area.
People and the Past (Learns about how things and people change over time)	22. Observes objects and events with curiosity 25. Explores cause and effect 29. Arranges objects in a series 31. Shows awareness of time concepts and sequence 35. Takes on pretend roles and situations	Invite grandparents to talk about their lives as children. Ask children to bring in pictures of themselves as a baby or an article of their baby clothing. Talk about how they have changed. Explore toys from long ago. Teach children games you played as a child.

The Arts

The arts are a natural part of children's experience. Children love using their bodies and materials to design, create, and explore. They mix paints; pound and shape clay; build structures with blocks, boxes, and Legos; dance; dramatize stories; clap rhythms; sing chants and songs. When children *do* art, they also think and solve problems:

- ❋ How can I make really dark purple?
- ❋ How do I make the clay softer?
- ❋ How do I put stairs on my building?
- ❋ How can I make my voice sound like a troll?
- ❋ How can I clap and sing at the same time?
- ❋ How can I use clay to make the boat I've drawn?

When the arts are an important part of an early childhood program, children gain valuable skills and knowledge.

They use a variety of media for communication and expression. Art is a symbolic language. It provides a way for children to understand and interpret the events in their lives. Through repeated experiences in the arts, children strengthen their ability to communicate their ideas, thoughts, and feelings.

They develop aesthetic knowledge and appreciation for many forms of expression. When children create, design, make, or perform—when they are artists—they gain an appreciation for the creative work of others and for their own. As they figure out how to make things happen in a particular way, children develop a deeper understanding of color, line, shape, balance, pattern, rhythm, movement, and texture.

They solve problems using various media. As children experiment with art materials, they solve problems. A child who looks at the picture she has drawn of a puppy and wants to recreate it in clay must figure out how to turn a two-dimensional picture into a three-dimensional figure. A child who wants to devise a new movement, make up new words to a song, or decide on ways to act out a character is also solving problems.

They learn about the world around them through their senses. The arts allow children to sharpen their ability to learn through their senses. Sensory learning is important in view of recent brain research that indicates that each sensory experience creates connections between brain cells. Repeated experiences solidify these connections. Thus, the arts provide an excellent opportunity to help wire children's brains for successful learning.

They develop an understanding of themselves and others. As children learn about art in different cultures and different eras, they become aware of people's lives, beliefs, and ways of expressing themselves. Whether they use musical instruments from different parts of the world or dramatize folktales or stories from another country, they are gaining a deeper understanding of their own culture and others.

Content of the Arts

In 1994, the Consortium of National Arts Education Associations developed the *National Standards for Arts Education: What Every Young American Should Know and Be Able to Do in the Arts.*[14] It organized standards for children in kindergarten through twelfth grade into four content areas:

* Dance
* Music
* Theater (Performing Arts)
* Visual Arts

To provide more direction for early childhood educators, the Task Force on Children's Learning and the Arts: Birth to Age Eight developed *Young Children and the Arts: Making Creative Connections.*[15] This document provides a framework for linking principles of child development with the arts.

Much of the content of the arts is emphasized throughout *The Creative Curriculum.* The chapter on Art provides guidance on the **visual arts.** The chapter on Music and Movement instructs teachers on how to provide appropriate experiences in **music** and **dance.** Throughout the *Curriculum,* we emphasize the important role of symbolic and pretend play. Components of the **theater** (performing arts) standards can be found in the house corner, the block corner, the library corner, and the music and movement area. In addition, group-time activities provide opportunities for dramatizations.

Objectives that focus on **Dance**

3. Recognizes own feelings and manages them appropriately
14. Demonstrates basic locomotor skills (running, jumping, hopping, galloping)
15. Shows balance while moving
30. Recognizes patterns and can repeat them
35. Takes on pretend roles and situations
37. Makes and interprets representations
40. Understands and follows oral directions

Dance

Young children are natural movers—they "think with their bodies" well before they think with words. When children are encouraged to use their bodies to express ideas, to respond to different rhythmic patterns, and to vary their responses to different musical phrases, they learn about the body's ability to move and use time and space in many different ways.

---

[14] *National Standards for Arts Education: What Every Young American Should Know and Be Able to Do in the Arts.* Reston, VA: Consortium of National Arts Education Associations, 1994.
[15] *Young Children and the Arts: Making Creative Connections.* Washington, DC: Arts Education Partnership, 1998.

When you include movement activities in the children's daily schedule, you are addressing dance. You can further a child's development in the area of dance:

❋ Teach new vocabulary words associated with movement such as *smooth, jerky, gallop,* and *glide.*

❋ Encourage creative thinking ("How would a snake move?" "First listen to the music. Then show me how your body wants to move.").

❋ Join in when a child is dancing and imitate the child's movements.

Music

Music literacy develops when children can listen to and interact with many kinds of music. This means that programs should provide opportunities to play with musical instruments, to learn and make up songs, to listen to recordings, and to talk about sounds. When preschool children explore instruments on their own, create melodies, learn songs as a group, and make up songs, they develop awareness of different kinds of music and become comfortable with different forms of musical expression.

Here are ways you can support children's learning in music:

❋ Set up a music and movement area where children can explore instruments, listen to a wide variety of music, and create music on their own.

❋ Introduce children to new words during music—*rhythm, beat, steady, fast, slow, loud, soft, lullaby, polka, country,* etc.

❋ Describe how a song makes you feel ("I always feel so sleepy when I hear this lullaby." "This song makes me want to stand up and start marching!").

❋ Use musical instruments in your group-time activities.

❋ Expose children to different kinds of music—*classical, jazz, country, rock, polka,* etc.

❋ Teach children songs that might be familiar to their families—folk songs, ballads—so they can sing together.

❋ Teach songs from the cultures of children in your classroom.

Objectives that focus on Music

3. Recognizes own feelings and manages them appropriately
25. Explores cause and effect
30. Recognizes patterns and can repeat them
31. Shows awareness of time concepts and sequence
34. Uses numbers and counting
35. Takes on pretend roles and situations
38. Hears and discriminates the sounds of language
39. Expresses self using words and expanded sentences
40. Understands and follows oral directions

Objectives that focus on Theater

3. Recognizes own feelings and manages them appropriately
11. Recognizes the feelings of others and responds appropriately
22. Observes objects and events with curiosity
31. Shows awareness of time concepts and sequence
32. Shows awareness of position in space
35. Takes on pretend roles and situations
38. Hears and discriminates the sounds of language
39. Expresses self using words and expanded sentences
40. Understands and follows oral directions

Theater (Performing Arts)

Drama is telling a story through action or dialogue. Preschool children recognize that movement can communicate messages and represent actions. During the preschool years, children learn through pretend play to pantomime actions such as eating, swimming, or driving a car. They also learn to express feelings and emotions as they play the roles of parent, firefighter, or superhero.

Dramatization also has a direct impact on other areas, such as language and literacy. In *Preventing Reading Difficulties in Young Children*[16] the writers report that children benefit from play-based instruction in which they invent dramatic play scenarios. This kind of sociodramatic play not only increases oral language use and enables children to practice storytelling skills, but it also offers a challenge for children to work together to negotiate their play ideas. These skills are closely related to the development of reading comprehension.

To encourage dramatization, you can:

❉ Provide props that will inspire children to act out different roles. Elaborate costumes are not necessary. Pretty pieces of fabric can be turned into capes, shawls, aprons, blankets, etc.
❉ Observe children as they are engaged in dramatic play. Make a comment or ask a question about what you see happening. At times children may invite you into their play as a participant.
❉ After reading a story, use props to help children act out the story.
❉ Play pantomime games during circle time.

Objectives that focus on Visual Arts

3. Recognizes own feelings and manages them appropriately
7. Respects and cares for classroom environment and materials
19. Controls small muscles in hands
21. Uses tools for writing and drawing
22. Observes objects and events with curiosity
25. Explores cause and effect
30. Recognizes patterns and can repeat them
32. Shows awareness of position in space
37. Makes and interprets representations

Visual Arts

The visual arts in preschool include painting; drawing; making collages; modeling and sculpting with clay or other materials; building; making puppets; weaving and stitching; and printmaking with stamps, blocks, or rubbings. Children benefit from opportunities to work with different kinds of paint and paper; draw with crayons, markers, and chalk; put things together with paste and glue; cut with scissors; mold playdough; and clean up with mops, sponges, and brooms. The more exposure children have to all kinds of materials—and to adults who talk about different ways to use the materials—the more children become able to express their ideas through the visual arts.

Not only do the visual arts provide a way of encouraging creativity, but they also provide a way to gain deeper understandings about the world. Children learn to draw at the same time they are drawing to learn. After exploring and learning how to use different

16 *Preventing Reading Difficulties in Young Children*, pp. 183-184.

materials—markers, clay, collage, wire, wood—children can use these materials to represent what they have learned about a topic. When a child recreates a drawing she has made, such as a pet cat, and tries to make it with another medium such as with clay or papier mâché, she has to think about different perspectives.

To help children learn more about the visual arts, you can:

❄ Teach them how to use different art tools and materials.

❄ Use new vocabulary words during art explorations—texture, pastel, knead, collage.

❄ Ask open-ended questions that will further their problem-solving abilities ("What do you think will happen if you try to tape the wood together?").

❄ Talk about what you see the child doing ("You made a red border around your picture").

❄ Use words to encourage and support a child's efforts ("You really took your time this morning creating this sculpture. Where shall we display it?").

❄ Display children's artwork prominently in the classroom.

How the Components of the Arts Are Addressed in
The Creative Curriculum®

COMPONENTS	CREATIVE CURRICULUM OBJECTIVES	WHAT TEACHERS DO
Dance (Learns about the body's ability to move and use time and space in different ways)	3. Recognizes own feelings and manages them appropriately 14. Demonstrates basic locomotor skills (running, jumping, hopping, galloping) 15. Shows balance while moving 30. Recognizes patterns and can repeat them 35. Takes on pretend roles and situations 37. Makes and interprets representations 40. Understands and follows oral directions	Offer children scarves and streamers to use as they dance to music. Invite children to move like the animals they saw at the zoo. Play different kinds of music that inspire children to move quickly (polka) or slowly (lullaby or spiritual).
Music (Develops an awareness of different kinds of music and becomes comfortable with different forms of musical expression)	3. Recognizes own feelings and manages them appropriately 25. Explores cause and effect 30. Recognizes patterns and can repeat them 31. Shows awareness of time concepts and sequence 34. Uses numbers and counting 35. Takes on pretend roles and situations 38. Hears and discriminates the sounds of language 39. Expresses self using words and expanded sentences 40. Understands and follows oral directions	Encourage children to try making different sounds with musical instruments. Play musical games such as "Ring around the Rosy" or "Farmer in the Dell." Create songs or chants while pounding clay. Describe how music makes you feel ("That music makes me think of a parade"). Clap different rhythmic patterns to music. Participate in and encourage children's pretend play.
Theater (Communicates a message or story through action or dialogue)	3. Recognizes own feelings and manages them appropriately 11. Recognizes the feelings of others and responds appropriately 22. Observes objects and events with curiosity 31. Shows awareness of time concepts and sequence 32. Shows awareness of position in space 35. Takes on pretend roles and situations 38. Hears and discriminates the sounds of language 39. Expresses self using words and expanded sentences 40. Understands and follows oral directions	Gather props and invite children to act out familiar stories such as Goldilocks and the Three Bears. Have children show you facial expressions of someone who is happy, sad, angry, tired, excited, or scared. Provide puppets and props.

How the Components of the Arts Are Addressed in *The Creative Curriculum*®

COMPONENTS	CREATIVE CURRICULUM OBJECTIVES	WHAT TEACHERS DO
Visual Arts (Uses a variety of media for communication and expression; solves problems using art materials; appreciates many forms of art)	3. Recognizes own feelings and manages them appropriately 7. Respects and cares for classroom environment and materials 19. Controls small muscles in hands 21. Uses tools for writing and drawing 22. Observes objects and events with curiosity 25. Explores cause and effect 30. Recognizes patterns and can repeat them 32. Shows awareness of position in space 37. Makes and interprets representations	Provide a variety of materials children can use to represent their ideas—markers, crayons, paints, clay, collage, wire, wood scraps. Talk about illustration techniques in books, such as Leo Leonni's torn paper pictures. Provide materials in the art center for children to experiment. Add mirrors to the art area and encourage children to look at their facial features when they draw people. Encourage children to draw pictures to show what they have learned.

Technology

When you hear the word *technology*, the first thought that may come to mind is computers. But technology is more than that. Think about all of the ways you use technology each day. Do you use an alarm clock? A coffee pot? A hair dryer or curling iron? Television or radio? A car? A microwave? A computer? So often we take technology for granted, but it's hard to imagine life without it.

Over the centuries, people have used technology—tools, machines, materials, techniques, and sources of power—to make work easier and to solve problems. When children explore how things work, they are learning about technology. They are solving technological problems when they figure out what kind of tools they need to build a structure using wood scraps. Using this broad definition of technology, you can see how it can be integrated into all aspects of the preschool classroom.

As you have read throughout this book, young children learn about the world around them in two ways: through hands-on, active exploration with materials and through interactions with adults and peers. In their explorations with materials, they pile blocks, mold clay, sift sand, and pretend play. They use all of their senses to form concepts about their world. Just as these materials provide different ways of exploring the world, so does technology. When children sing songs into a tape recorder or create colored lines on the screen by dragging a mouse, they are using newer tools for discovery.

For children with disabilities, the use of technology opens new avenues for learning. A child who is unable to speak can use communication devices to interact with others. A child who is physically impaired can use switches to control battery-operated toys. Special assistive devices allow children with a handicapping condition to have equal access to the learning environment.

How Young Children Explore Technology

Anytime you learn something new, you go through certain phases in the process of understanding and using what you have learned. In *Reaching Potentials*, Bredekamp and Rosegrant describe the learning cycle as having four phases: awareness, exploration, inquiry, and utilization.[17] Using this model, you can think about how young children learn about technology.

Awareness—Children are immersed in a technological world. They watch adults use all kinds of appliances—can opener, mixer, blender, oven, iron, vacuum cleaner, or washer and dryer—to make household jobs easier. They see family members using telephones, stereos, and perhaps a computer. In their community, they see traffic lights changing colors, a tow truck hauling away a car, or a jackhammer breaking concrete. At the supermarket, they see a door open automatically, hear music through a speaker system, and watch the cashier scan groceries.

Exploration—Young children love to find out how things work and to imitate what they see others do. As they explore technological tools, they learn about cause and effect:

❈ If I move this mouse, a line appears on the computer screen.
❈ If I press these keys, letters and numbers appear on the screen.
❈ If I push this button, I'll hear music from the tape recorder.
❈ If I turn this key, the wind-up toy moves.

Children use all their senses to construct knowledge and understanding about the tools that make our lives easier, more interesting, and, often, more fun.

Inquiry—During this stage of learning about technology, children investigate further and ask questions that will help them understand how things work. They realize that people control technology. A person has to do *something* to make this tool work. They ask questions such as, "How can I draw a circle on the computer?" or "How can I erase my picture?"

17 Bredekamp, Sue, and Teresa Rosegrant. *Reaching Potentials: Appropriate Curriculum and Assessment for Young Children, Volume 1*. Washington, DC: NAEYC, 1992.

Utilization—Once children have become aware of a technological tool, and have explored and investigated it further to make some generalizations, they can start to use that tool in a meaningful way in their everyday life. They begin to select the right tool to accomplish a specific task. If they want to weigh their rocks, they use a balance or bathroom scale. If they want to see something up close, they use a magnifying glass. If they want to create a picture, they can use crayons, paint, or a drawing program on the computer. And if they want to write words about their creations, they can use pencils, pens, or a word processing program.

The Content of Technology

The National Educational Technology Standards for Students[18] outline the skills, concepts, knowledge, and attitudes that children in preschool through grade twelve should have the opportunity to demonstrate. Not only do the standards focus on basic skills related to computers, but they also focus on using technology to communicate, to learn new information, to solve problems, and to create. Equally important, the standards also stress social skills, such as working cooperatively with peers and using technology responsibly.

As we researched state standards for technology, we noted several different approaches. Some states have separate standards for technology, while others embed technology within the different content areas. Drawing from the national, state, and local standards in technology, we have summarized the big ideas that are appropriate to preschool.

Awareness of Technology

As preschoolers begin to explore the world around them, they can examine how technology is used in their homes, at school, and at family members' work sites. They can name the tools and machines they use every day and think about how tasks might be accomplished if this equipment were not available. They can also learn firsthand how people use technology to do their jobs.

One way to promote technology literacy is to have conversations with children about the technology they see and experience in their everyday lives. Ask them open-ended questions that will guide them to think about how technology makes our lives better.

> Objectives that focus on
> **Awareness of Technology**
>
> 22. Observes objects and events with curiosity
> 35. Takes on pretend roles and situations
> 36. Makes believe with objects
> 39. Expresses self using words and expanded sentences
> 42. Asks questions

* "I wonder how we would open this can if we didn't have a can opener."
* "How do you think Mrs. Hewlett's voice comes through the intercom on the wall?"

---

[18] International Society for Technology Education. *National Educational Technology Standards for Students.* Eugene, OR: ISTE, 1998.

❉ "Look at the picture of my nephew I received on my e-mail today. He lives far, far away."

❉ "Can you think of a way that we can get the books into our loft? Carrying them while you climb the stairs can be dangerous."

Basic Operations and Concepts

Through hands-on exploration, children begin to learn how to use technology. Your task is to introduce various technologies to children and explain how to care for these tools and use them safely.

The basics for using computers include how to turn on the computer, start up a program, navigate through software that is developmentally appropriate, and exit the program. *The Creative Curriculum* describes in detail how to introduce children to computers and how to interact with children so that they can acquire knowledge and concepts about this technology. Children learn computer terminology, such as mouse, cursor, disk, CD-ROM, and keyboard.

Objectives that focus on Basic Operations and Concepts

5. Demonstrates self-direction and independence
7. Respects and cares for classroom environment and materials
19. Controls small muscles in hands
22. Observes objects and events with curiosity
23. Approaches problems flexibly
25. Explores cause and effect
37. Makes and interprets representations
46. Demonstrates knowledge of the alphabet
47. Uses emerging reading skills to make meaning from print

Technology Tools

There are different forms of technology—tape recorders, computers, digital cameras, calculators, VCRs. By using various forms of technology, children learn that each serves a different purpose.

❉ To draw a picture, I can use crayons, markers, paint, or a computer drawing program.
❉ To write a story, I can use a pencil, pens, markers, or a word processing program.
❉ To find a picture of the bird, I can use books, photo albums, software program with pictures of birds, or a web site on birds.

Objectives that focus on Technology Tools

22. Observes objects and events with curiosity
23. Approaches problems flexibly
25. Explores cause and effect
26. Applies knowledge or experience to a new context
36. Makes believe with objects

People and Technology

Because technology is part of everyday life and is often taken for granted, it is important for children to understand that people, including themselves, control technology. For example, children can control how they navigate through a software program, change the volume on a tape recorder, or flip a light switch. They can watch you connect the various components of a computer. On a field trip, they can see how people control technology in the world of work.

An important component of technology is learning how to use it responsibly and safely. Children learn how to care for the equipment and use it appropriately. They learn how to handle floppy disks and CD-ROMs properly. They learn how to exit a software program before turning the computer off. They learn how to keep things away from equipment that might damage it.

Young children can also learn how people can work together to use technology. A group of children can solve problems together on the computer. If they can't figure out how to do something, they find a friend or adult who can help them.

> ### Objectives that focus on **People and Technology**
>
> 5. Demonstrates self-direction and independence
> 22. Observes objects and events with curiosity
> 23. Approaches problems flexibly
> 25. Explores cause and effect
> 26. Applies knowledge or experience to a new context

How the Components of Technology Are Addressed in *The Creative Curriculum®*

COMPONENTS	*CREATIVE CURRICULUM* OBJECTIVES	WHAT TEACHERS DO
Awareness of Technology (Gains awareness of technology as a tool for finding information, communicating, and creating)	22. Observes objects and events with curiosity 35. Takes on pretend roles and situations 36. Makes believe with objects 39. Expresses self using words and expanded sentences 42. Asks questions	Offer toy cell phones, cameras, microphones for children to use during play. Point out how technology is used while on field trips ("The computer helps the firefighter see a map leading him to the fire"). Take videos of children during play and replay them.
Basic Operations and Concepts (Learns basic skills to operate technology; uses appropriate terminology to communicate about technology)	5. Demonstrates self-direction and independence 7. Respects and cares for classroom environment and materials 19. Controls small muscles in hands 22. Observes objects and events with curiosity 23. Approaches problems flexibly 25. Explores cause and effect 37. Makes and interprets representations 46. Demonstrates knowledge of the alphabet 47. Uses emerging reading skills to make meaning from print	Show children how to use a mouse, keyboard, or touch screen to operate a computer. Teach children about the picture cues (icons) that will help them navigate through a software program. Use computer terminology when showing children how to use a software program ("I'm going to paste the picture here"). Teach children how to exit a program before turning off the computer.
Technology Tools (Understands that there are different tools of technology, and they can be used in a variety of ways)	22. Observes objects and events with curiosity 23. Approaches problems flexibly 25. Explores cause and effect 26. Applies knowledge or experience to a new context 36. Makes believe with objects	Encourage children to retell a story into a tape recorder and ask others to listen. Set up a drawing program so children can create a picture to represent what they have learned. Show children how they can use a simple word processing program to type their names or words. Provide tools such as magnifying glasses, balance scales, binoculars to explore and investigate.
People and Technology (Understands that technology is controlled by people; uses technology safely and responsibly; works collaboratively while using technology)	5. Demonstrates self-direction and independence 22. Observes objects and events with curiosity 23. Approaches problems flexibly 25. Explores cause and effect 26. Applies knowledge or experience to a new context	Show children how to drag a mouse to create a line in a paint program. Teach children how to operate a tape recorder. Encourage children to work with a friend to figure out how to navigate through a software program. Develop rules with the children for using the computer safely and properly.

In this chapter we described the content standards for literacy, math, science, social studies, the arts, and technology and pulled out the key components useful to teachers of 3- to 5-year-old children. We showed you how these components relate to the goals and objectives of *The Creative Curriculum* and identified a wide variety of activities and learning experiences children need to move successfully along the Developmental Continuum. We conclude by returning you to the *Curriculum*.

Chapter III
Returning to the Curriculum

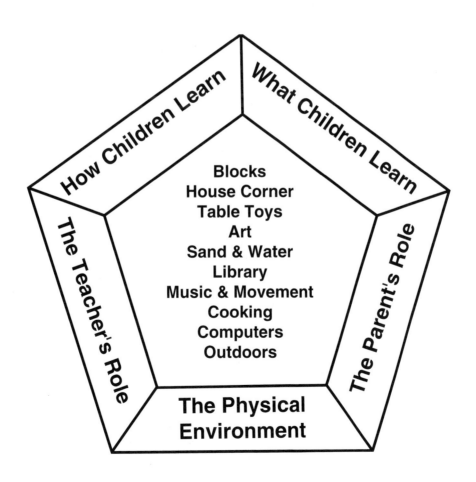

In this book we describe *The Creative Curriculum Developmental Continuum* showing the expected steps in development for 3- to 5-year-olds. We describe the content standards for literacy, math, science, social studies, the arts, and technology and show how an understanding of content helps you learn what to teach. Now we conclude by returning to the *Curriculum* itself.

Why do we do this? As a teacher, you make countless decisions every day—decisions about your daily program and how to individualize instruction for each child. *The Creative Curriculum* gives you a framework for decision making, based on what you know about how children learn, what you want children to learn, what type of setting will promote learning, how to guide children's learning, and how to support and involve families. We illustrate this decision-making framework in the *Curriculum,* as shown below.

How Children Learn

What Children Learn

The Teacher's Role

The Parent's Role

Blocks
House Corner
Table Toys
Art
Sand & Water
Library
Music & Movement
Cooking
Computers
Outdoors

The Physical Environment

Using *The Creative Curriculum* framework helps you answer questions such as the following:

❀ Does the room arrangement support positive behavior?

❀ How can I help children to use materials more carefully and clean up?

❀ Are children learning through their play?

❀ How can we make transitions occur more smoothly?

❀ Is this a good time to introduce new props, learning materials, books, or toys?

❀ How can I encourage children to do more writing?

❀ What would be a good topic for our next study?

The Creative Curriculum shows how to promote children's development and learning in interest areas, during daily routines, by planning studies that integrate learning in the content areas, and by individualizing for each child.

Using Interest Areas to Promote Learning

One of the primary ways that teachers use *The Creative Curriculum* is as a resource in setting up attractive, well-organized, and rich interest areas. Throughout the *Curriculum*, we offer ideas on how to select and arrange materials, and how to interact with children so that they acquire knowledge and skills. The charts that follow provide a few examples of ways to address literacy, math, science, social studies, the arts, and technology in each of the ten interest areas and during group times and daily routines.

How Teachers Use Interest Areas to Address Content

	Blocks	House Corner	Table Toys	Art
Literacy	✻ Have paper, markers, and tape available for children to make signs for block buildings. ✻ Hang charts and pictures with words at children's eye level.	✻ Include books and magazines in the house corner. ✻ Introduce uses of print (shopping lists, receipts, message writing, etc.).	✻ Talk about colors, shapes, pictures in a lotto game. ✻ Provide matching games for visual discrimination.	✻ Invite children to dictate stories to go with their artwork. ✻ Share books about famous artists and their work with children.
Math	✻ Suggest clean-up activities that involve sorting by shape and size. ✻ Use language of comparison such as taller, shorter, the same length.	✻ Add telephones, menus, and other items with numbers on them. ✻ Participate in play, talking about prices, addresses, and times of day.	✻ Provide collections for sorting, classifying, and graphing. ✻ Have children extend patterns with colored cubes, beads, etc.	✻ Use terms of comparison (the piece of yarn is longer than your arm). ✻ Provide empty containers of various shapes for creating junk sculptures.
Science	✻ Talk with children about size, weight, and balance. ✻ Encourage children to experiment with momentum using ramps, balls, and marbles.	✻ Introduce props such as a stethoscope or binoculars. ✻ Model hygiene skills by washing "babies" or dishes.	✻ Talk about balance and weight as children use table blocks. ✻ Sort, classify, and graph nature items such as rocks, leaves, twigs, and shells.	✻ Describe the properties of materials as they interact (wet, dry, gooey, sticky). ✻ Use water and brushes for outdoor painting so children can explore evaporation.
Social Studies	✻ Include block people who represent a range of jobs and cultures. ✻ Display pictures of buildings in the neighborhood.	✻ Include props related to different kinds of jobs. ✻ Add multicultural dolls and props such as cooking utensils, foods, and clothing.	✻ Select puzzles and other materials that include diverse backgrounds and jobs. ✻ Play board games that require cooperation, following rules, and taking turns.	✻ Include various shades of skin tone paint, crayons, markers, and construction paper. ✻ Encourage children to paint and draw what they saw on a field trip.
The Arts	✻ Encourage children to build props, such as a bridge for *The Three Billy Goats Gruff* for dramatization. ✻ Display artwork posters that include geometric shapes and patterns.	✻ Display children's art work or art posters in the house corner decor. ✻ Provide props for children to dramatize different roles.	✻ Include materials that have different art elements (pattern or texture matching, color games, etc.). ✻ Add building toys that encourage creativity such as Legos, Tinker-toys, etc.	✻ Provide different media for children to explore clay, paint, collage, construction, etc. ✻ Invite a local artist to share his/her work and to join children in the art area.
Technology	✻ Include ramps, wheels, and pulleys. ✻ Take pictures (using digital, instant, or regular cameras) of block structures and display in the area.	✻ Include technology props such as old cameras, computers, keyboards, micro-phones, etc. ✻ Encourage children to explore how tools work—eggbeaters, can openers, etc.	✻ Add toys (gears, marble mazes, etc.) that encourage children to explore how things work. ✻ Use a light table for exploring transparent shapes.	✻ Include recyclable materials for children to create an invention. ✻ Use technological tools for creating items such as a potter's wheel or spin art.

How Teachers Use Interest Areas to Address Content

	Sand and Water	Library	Music/Movement	Cooking
Literacy	✱ Add literacy props such as letter molds or road signs to the sand table. ✱ Encourage children to use words to describe how the sand and water feel.	✱ Keep a rich assortment of good children's books on display. ✱ Set up a writing area with pens, markers, pencils, paper, stamps, envelopes, etc.	✱ Write words to a favorite song on a chart. ✱ Have children use instruments for the sound effects in stories.	✱ Use pictures and words on recipe cards. ✱ Talk about words and letters on the food containers during a cooking activity.
Math	✱ Provide measuring cups, spoons, containers of various sizes. ✱ Ask estimation questions ("How many cups will take to fill the yellow container?").	✱ Add number stamps to the writing area. ✱ Include books about math concepts: size, number, comparisons, shapes, etc.	✱ Play percussion games emphasizing pattern: softer, louder. ✱ Use language that describes spatial relationships—under, over, around, through.	✱ Use a timer in cooking. ✱ Provide measuring cups and spoons.
Science	✱ Make bubble solution and provide different kinds of bubble-blowing tools. ✱ Put out magnifying glasses and sifters so children can examine different kinds of sand.	✱ Include books about pets, plants, bodies, water, inventions, etc. ✱ Provide a variety of objects for experimentation with floating and sinking.	✱ Set out bottles with varied amounts of water so children can investigate the sounds they produce. ✱ Use a tape recorder to record children's voices; play back for children to identify.	✱ Encourage children to taste, smell, touch, listen and observe at each step of the cooking process. ✱ Discuss how heating and freezing changes substances.
Social Studies	✱ Invite children to describe roads and tunnels created in sand. ✱ Hang pictures of bodies of water (rivers, oceans, lakes, streams) near the water table.	✱ Include books that reflect diversity of culture and gender. ✱ Show children how to use nonfiction books, picture dictionaries, and encyclopedias to find information on a topic.	✱ Show videotapes reflecting songs and dances of many cultures and languages. ✱ Include instruments from different cultures.	✱ Encourage parents to bring in recipes reflecting family cultures. ✱ Visit stores that sell foods of different cultures.
The Arts	✱ Create sand sculptures; display photographs of sand sculptures created by artists. ✱ Use tools for drawing in wet sand.	✱ Talk about art techniques used by illustrators (e.g., torn paper collage by Leo Lionni). ✱ Include children's informational books of famous artwork.	✱ Provide a variety of musical instruments to explore. ✱ Add scarves, streamers, and costumes to encourage dancing.	✱ Encourage children to be creative while preparing their snacks. ✱ Dramatize foods being cooked—a kernel of popcorn being popped; cheese melting.
Technology	✱ Include props with moving parts at the water table—such as water wheels, eggbeaters, pump, etc. ✱ Use toy dump trucks, loaders, cranes for outdoor sand play.	✱ Set up a listening area with books on tape. ✱ Include books about how things work.	✱ Add an electronic keyboard that produces different sounds. ✱ Include tape recorders, CD player, headphones, etc.	✱ Cook a recipe in a microwave and conventional oven and compare cooking times. ✱ Examine how different kitchen gadgets work.

How Teachers Use Interest Areas to Address Content

	Computers	Outdoors	Group Times	Daily Routines
Literacy	✳ Have paper, markers, and tape available for children to make signs for block buildings. ✳ Use a drawing or simple word processing program to make a book.	✳ Bring colored chalk and other writing materials outside. ✳ Have children observe street signs in the neighborhood.	✳ Lead discussions and teach children how to talk and listen to others. ✳ Read, tell, and dramatize stories every day.	✳ Label children's cubbies and belongings with their names. ✳ Use pictures and words to create a daily schedule on chart paper. ✳ Have children sign in each day.
Math	✳ Include software that focuses on number concepts, patterning, problem solving, shapes, etc. ✳ Use a drawing program to create patterns.	✳ Have children look for patterns in nature. ✳ Invite children to make collections on a walk, then sort, classify, and graph the items collected.	✳ Count the number of girls and boys present; talk about which group is larger and which is smaller. ✳ Create graphs describing characteristics/preferences (e.g., favorite snack, types of shoes).	✳ Have children count the number of cups and napkins needed during snack time. ✳ Use math vocabulary throughout the day ("Would you like half a cup of juice?").
Science	✳ Have children observe cause and effect by hitting a key or dragging a mouse. ✳ Allow children to observe as you connect computer components.	✳ Take pictures of a tree the children see every day and discuss how it changes during the year. ✳ Have children feel their heartbeat after running or exercising.	✳ Talk about the weather and the signs of seasons changing. ✳ Conduct simple experiments together.	✳ Take turns feeding the classroom pet or watering the plants and talk about why we do this. ✳ Have a child check the weather and talk about what kind of clothing to wear outdoors.
Social Studies	✳ Encourage children to work cooperatively on software related to the topic being studied. ✳ Develop rules for computer use with the children and post them in the area.	✳ Take many trips in the neighborhood and talk about what you see. ✳ Invite children to make maps of outdoor environments using chalk on concrete.	✳ Have children dictate letters to community helpers—firefighters, mail carriers, police officers, etc. ✳ Hold class meetings for sharing and problem solving.	✳ Model good manners during snack and mealtimes. ✳ Have conversations with children about their family activities.
The Arts	✳ Include drawing and painting software. ✳ Include software that allows children to create musical tunes.	✳ Bring art materials outdoors for creating pictures and sculptures. ✳ Provide streamers and scarves for outdoor dance and movement activities.	✳ Play a variety of music styles (classical, country, rock, ragtime) and have children move in different ways. ✳ Act out stories or play pantomime games.	✳ Play soft, classical music during rest time. ✳ Sing songs or play music during daily transitions.
Technology	✳ Set up a computer area with open-ended software programs for children to use. ✳ Add an inexpensive camera to the computer and allow children to see themselves on the screen.	✳ Point out examples of technology while on a walk in the neighborhood. ✳ Provide tools for investigating outdoors such as magnifying glasses, binoculars, periscopes, etc.	✳ Introduce children to new software programs during group time. ✳ Have children dictate an e-mail message to a family member, then read the response.	✳ Talk about the technology children see and hear each day—intercom, bells, computers, etc. ✳ Take photos of children and families to display in the class room.

How Studies Integrate Learning

The Creative Curriculum describes a way to tie content together through planning and implementing *studies*. Today, the literature uses the terms *studies* or *projects*. In the past, the literature sometimes spoke of *themes*. Lilian Katz and Sylvia Chard introduced the "project approach," which they define as "children's in-depth investigations of various topics—ideally, topics worthy of children's time and energy."[19] Regardless of the term, the approach we describe involves organizing the daily curriculum in a way that is both meaningful and exciting for children. Specifically, projects or studies provide a way to:

* explore a topic in-depth through hands-on investigation and exploration;
* acquire knowledge in the content areas;
* apply skills in a meaningful way;
* explore real-world problems;
* engage and challenge all students;
* encourage cooperative learning; and
* involve families in children's learning.

A good study topic also enables you to address all areas of development:

Social/Emotional—When children work cooperatively on a study, they feel a part of the group and develop friendships. They assume responsibilities and develop independence as they complete tasks. They experience the pride of making discoveries or completing a model to share. And because they are interested in the topic, they are motivated to learn.

Physical—Children can use their bodies to explore any topic under consideration. Whether it's digging a garden or sorting small rocks with tweezers, children develop their large and small muscles.

Cognitive—In a study, children acquire new knowledge and understandings about a topic through meaningful activities that take place in and around the classroom. Because the curriculum content begins with the familiar environment, children can apply previously learned skills to new situations. They use their skills to explore or investigate a topic in depth.

Language—As children learn new words, discuss a topic, or dramatize an event, they develop and enrich language skills. They learn how to ask questions when they interview an expert. They use books, magazines, and brochures to research a topic. Children communicate what they have learned to others by writing or dictating stories and experiences.

---

19 Katz, Lilian G., and Sylvia C. Chard, "Issues in Selecting Topics for Projects," ERIC DIGEST. Champaign, IL: Clearinghouse on Elementary and Early Childhood Education. 1998.

Throughout the study you can observe and record children's comments and questions, their involvement with projects, their successes, and their confusions. You can collect samples of children's work, photographs of their constructions, and photocopies of their writing. Using this documentation and reflecting on children's progress relative to the Developmental Continuum will help you plan and individualize instruction for each child.

An Example of a Study: The Post Office

The Jolly Postman or Other People's Letters by Janet and Allan Ahlberg is a favorite book in Mr. Gomez's preschool class. In this book, a postman delivers letters to several famous fairy-tale characters such as the Big Bad Wolf, Cinderella, and the Three Bears. Each letter can be removed from its envelope page and read separately. After reading the book to the class, Mr. Gomez observed children attempting to read it in the library corner and talking about the letters written to the fairy-tale characters.

To build their interest, Mr. Gomez added literacy materials such as envelopes, stamps, postcards, and stationery to the writing area of the library corner. Patrick, Juan, and Sara wrote letters and postcards for the Jolly Postman to deliver. Mr. Gomez noticed that children's play about mail delivery was beginning to emerge in other interest areas. Marianna and Derrick created a mailbag using paper and tape. Mandy and Juan made mailboxes out of old shoeboxes. Tony, Marcus, and Ann built a post office out of hollow blocks.

During group time, Mr. Gomez and the children talked about their play in the interest areas. He asked open-ended questions to find out what children already knew about the mail system:

- *"Have you ever received a letter in the mail?"*
- *"I wonder what happens to a letter after you drop it in a mailbox."*
- *"Why do you think this mark [postmark] is made on a stamp?"*
- *"What do you think would happen if you didn't put a stamp on a letter?"*

In the days and weeks that followed, Mr. Gomez continued to observe children during their play and to build on their interest by engaging in conversations and offering materials and ideas to extend their learning. The children went on a field trip to the post office at the beginning of their study to find out answers to their questions. They went again several weeks later when their work led to new questions. Children represented their learning by drawing pictures of postal vehicles and creating neighborhoods with blocks for mail delivery.

Mr. Gomez's role during the study was critical. He observed the children's play and found a topic that not only was of interest to them, but had educational potential, as well. Keeping in mind the developmental sequence of goals and objectives in *The Creative Curriculum* and key components of the content areas, he added materials to the environment that would deepen the children's understanding and provide opportunities to practice skills. As a result, the study connected content, teaching, and learning in a way that engaged children as learners.

Studies can be very short—a few days—or can extend over weeks or months. The chart on the next page shows you how content was addressed throughout the study of the post office.

A Study of the Post Office

Literacy	❋ Read books about the mail and the post office such as *A Letter to Amy* by Ezra Jack Keats. ❋ Look for and identify words on a mailbox or at the post office. ❋ Add literacy props related to the post office to be used in play: envelopes, stamps, stationery, and writing tools. ❋ Write letters to a sick classmate.	❋ Learn new vocabulary words about the post office (address, sort, scale, postage meter, package). ❋ Dictate letters and address envelopes to be mailed. ❋ Write a thank-you note to the postal carrier. ❋ Create signs for the classroom post office. ❋ Use stamps for "air mail," "first class," etc.
Math	❋ Weigh mail and packages. ❋ Sort and organize collections of stamps, greeting cards, or old postcards. ❋ Mail a letter and count the number of days it takes to arrive. ❋ Decide how many shoe boxes it would take to create a mailbox for each child.	❋ Visit post office to buy stamps. ❋ Use play money in classroom post office. ❋ Count letters to be mailed. ❋ Fold letters into shapes so they can fit in an envelope.
Science	❋ Use recycled materials for creating greeting cards. ❋ Take apart an old scale to find out how it works. ❋ Learn about the machines used for sorting mail at the post office.	❋ Find out what makes stamps and envelopes stick; make paste using flour and water. ❋ Look at and feel different kinds of paper (onionskin, card stock, glossy paper); figure out ways to move heavy packages.
Social Studies	❋ Find out about the jobs different people have at the post office. ❋ Take a neighborhood walk to mail letters. ❋ Learn social skills in classroom post office ("May I help you?" "Thank you" "Please come again"). ❋ Invite parents and grandparents to share a stamp or postcard collection.	❋ Compare how the mail is moved (by foot, trucks, planes). ❋ Find out how the visually impaired might create a letter using braille. ❋ Examine different kinds of mailboxes in an apartment, rural mailbox, in a post office, mail slots, etc.
The Arts	❋ Set up post office in dramatic play area for pretend play. ❋ Create stationery, postcards. ❋ Use props to retell stories such as *The Jolly Postman* by Janet and Allan Ahlberg.	❋ Paint cardboard boxes to become a mail truck. ❋ Play A Tisket, A Tasket. ❋ Pantomime different ways to move the mail (walking, flying, driving).
Technology	❋ Find out what tools are used at the post office. ❋ Use a word processing program to write letters on the computer. ❋ Use *The Jolly Postman* CD-ROM.	❋ Use a digital camera to take photographs on a field trip to the post office. ❋ Use a tape recorder to interview postal workers.

Individualizing the Curriculum

Finally, *The Creative Curriculum* emphasizes the importance of observing children to learn more about them and determine where they are in their development. Your observations will lead you to reflect on the best ways to respond, as well as how to adapt the *Curriculum* for individual children. Here are some examples of what you might learn from your observations of individual children and the kinds of questions you might ask yourself.

❋ Rashida has difficulty paying attention during storytime. Would it help if she sits near me? Are there other times of the day when she has difficulty paying attention?

❋ Manuel's approach to joining a group leads the other children to reject him. How can I teach him a more successful way to be accepted? Who might become his friend?

❋ Susie falls apart at naptime every day. What can we do to make this period of the day easier for her?

❋ Josie is all excited about her new kitten. How can we build on this new interest to promote her language and literacy skills?

❋ Devon has been building the same block structure for weeks. Is he stuck? How can we use his interest in block building to extend his learning?

❋ Derrick is not able to recognize the first letter of his name. How can I provide more opportunities for him to see his name used in a variety of ways and places throughout the day? I will need to help him focus on this.

❋ Jacob has been making patterns lately. Where is he in his development, and how can I help him to take the next step?

The Developmental Continuum enables you to answer your questions about individual children by helping you pinpoint where each child is in terms of a particular objective. In turn, this knowledge allows you to plan ways to move him or her to the next step. To show how this might work, let's suppose that your observations of Jacob show that he is at the midpoint on the Continuum (step II) for Objective 30, "Recognizes patterns and can repeat them." Here's what you might do with the information:

While working with Jacob in the table toy area, you watch him making a tower of interlocking cubes—red, white, red, white. To help Jacob move from working with simple patterns to ones that are more complex, you pick up another set of cubes and begin making a pattern using three colors. You say to Jacob, "What am I doing with my cubes?" Jacob replies, "You've got red, white, blue, red, white, blue, red, and white." You ask, "What comes next?" Jacob answers, "Blue," and you encourage him to add a blue cube to his structure.

Over the next few days, you notice that Jacob is beginning to work on more complex patterns. To further support Jacob's learning about patterns, you draw his attention to patterns in the environment. On the playground, you help Jacob observe a pattern in the fence and the design in the hedges. Gradually, Jacob starts making more complicated patterns both with table toys and in music.

The interest area chapters of *The Creative Curriculum* show how teachers observe children to decide how to respond in ways that promote learning. Once again, your familiarity with the goals and objectives makes this task easier by providing a focus for your observations and a way to identify where a child is in relation to *Curriculum* objectives. On the basis of what you learn, you can ask questions about how best to respond and identify teaching strategies that might work.

The following chart shows how this process might take place in the block area.

What Child Does	What Objectives Are Addressed	Questions to Ask Yourself	What You Might Do
Takes block away from another child.	Objective 4. Stands up for rights (Notice in which situations the child shares and respects rights of others, Objective 12)	Does she have the words to use to ask for the block? Is sharing difficult? Why? Do I have a sufficient number of blocks out?	Say to her, "It looks like you need more blocks. You don't need to take someone else's. We can find some for you on the shelf." Add to the supply of blocks.
Appears frustrated when blocks keep falling down while building on a carpet.	Objective 24. Shows persistence in approaching tasks Objective 37. Makes and interprets representations (Look for progress in Objective 25. Explores cause and effect)	How can I help him understand what's causing the problem? Do I have the right kind of surface for building?	Ask, "What do you think is causing the blocks to fall down?" Offer a suggestion: "What do you think might happen if you try to build on the hard floor?" Provide hard surfaces for building (cardboard, tile). Offer him paper and pencil to make a sign for his structure.
Says to another child, "No, this is not a house. This is a fire station."	Objective 37. Makes and interprets representations Objective 36. Makes believes with objects Objective 26. Applies knowledge or experience to a new context Objective 39. Expresses self using words and expanded sentences	What would help him to communicate what he has built? Is he ready to expand on his building?	Provide additional props such as fire trucks, people figures, child-size firefighter hats, or toy ambulance.
Puts blocks away without sorting.	Objective 7. Respects and cares for classroom environment and materials Objective 5. Demonstrates self-direction and independence (Look for progress on Objective 27. Classifies objects)	Does she notice the difference in size and shape of blocks? Have I clearly organized and labeled the shelves? Have I taught the children how to store the blocks?	Say, "Let's put away all the triangle blocks first. Can you find all the blocks that look like this?" Clearly label all the blocks and talk to the children about how they are arranged and why.

Conclusion

Our purpose in writing this book was to answer the three questions we posed in the beginning:

* ❀ How do you know if your program is effective and if children are learning?
* ❀ What kinds of experiences should children have during their early years that will help them develop the skills and motivation they need to become lifelong learners?
* ❀ How do teachers address content in a *Creative Curriculum* classroom?

The connection between content, teaching, and learning is often difficult to make and even more challenging to explain to people who need reassurance that children are truly learning—parents and administrators, funders, and the public. We have offered you tools and materials to determine areas in which each child is making progress, to plan based on what you learn, and to explain how and what children are learning through interest areas, group experiences, and daily life in the program. We hope we have reassured you that using an environmentally based, interactive, play-oriented approach is an effective way to help children acquire important skills and content, develop social competence—and to prepare them to become life-long learners.

Appendix A

The Creative Curriculum®
Goals and Objectives at a Glance

The Creative Curriculum® Goals and Objectives at a Glance

SOCIAL/EMOTIONAL DEVELOPMENT

Sense of Self

1. Shows ability to adjust to new situations
2. Demonstrates appropriate trust in adults
3. Recognizes own feelings and manages them appropriately
4. Stands up for rights

Responsibility for Self and Others

5. Demonstrates self-direction and independence
6. Takes responsibility for own well-being
7. Respects and cares for classroom environment and materials
8. Follows classroom routines
9. Follows classroom rules

Prosocial Behavior

10. Plays well with other children
11. Recognizes the feelings of others and responds appropriately
12. Shares and respects the rights of others
13. Uses thinking skills to resolve conflicts

PHYSICAL DEVELOPMENT

Gross Motor

14. Demonstrates basic locomotor skills (running, jumping, hopping, galloping)
15. Shows balance while moving
16. Climbs up and down
17. Pedals and steers a tricycle (or other wheeled vehicle)
18. Demonstrates throwing, kicking, and catching skills

Fine Motor

19. Controls small muscles in hands
20. Coordinates eye-hand movement
21. Uses tools for writing and drawing

COGNITIVE DEVELOPMENT

Learning and Problem Solving

22. Observes objects and events with curiosity
23. Approaches problems flexibly
24. Shows persistence in approaching tasks
25. Explores cause and effect
26. Applies knowledge or experience to a new context

Logical Thinking

27. Classifies objects
28. Compares/measures
29. Arranges objects in a series
30. Recognizes patterns and can repeat them
31. Shows awareness of time concepts and sequence
32. Shows awareness of position in space
33. Uses one-to-one correspondence
34. Uses numbers and counting

Representation and Symbolic Thinking

35. Takes on pretend roles and situations
36. Makes believe with objects
37. Makes and interprets representations

LANGUAGE DEVELOPMENT

Listening and Speaking

38. Hears and discriminates the sounds of language
39. Expresses self using words and expanded sentences
40. Understands and follows oral directions
41. Answers questions
42. Asks questions
43. Actively participates in conversations

Reading and Writing

44. Enjoys and values reading
45. Demonstrates understanding of print concepts
46. Demonstrates knowledge of the alphabet
47. Uses emerging reading skills to make meaning from print
48. Comprehends and interprets meaning from books and other texts
49. Understands the purpose of writing
50. Writes letters and words

©2001 Teaching Strategies, Inc. Washington, DC. Permission is granted to duplicate in programs implementing *The Creative Curriculum*.

Appendix B

Developmental Continuum
for Ages 3-5

SOCIAL/EMOTIONAL DEVELOPMENT

Sense of Self

Curriculum Objectives	Developmental Continuum for Ages 3-5			
		I	II	III
1. **Shows ability to adjust to new situations**	**Forerunners** Interacts with teachers when family member is nearby Is able to move away from family member; checks back occasionally ("social referencing")	Treats arrival and departure as routine parts of the day *e.g., says good-bye to family members without undue stress; accepts comfort from teacher*	Accepts changes in daily schedules and routines *e.g., eagerly participates in a field trip; accepts visitors to classroom*	Functions with increasing independence in school *e.g., readily goes to other parts of the building for scheduled activities; willingly delivers a message from classroom teacher to the office*
2. **Demonstrates appropriate trust in adults**	**Forerunners** Seeks to be near trusted adult as a "safe haven" Makes visual or physical contact with trusted adult for reassurance	Shows confidence in parents' and teachers' abilities to keep him/her safe and healthy *e.g., explores the indoor and outdoor environments without being fearful; summons adult when assistance is needed*	Regards parents and teachers as resources and positive role models *e.g., imitates parents going to work or at home during dramatic play; asks teacher's advice on how to saw a piece of wood in half*	Knows the difference between adults who can help (family members, friends, staff) and those who may not (strangers) *e.g., knows who is allowed to give her medicine; talks about why children shouldn't go anywhere with strangers*
3. **Recognizes own feelings and manages them appropriately**	**Forerunners** Cries to express displeasure Uses facial expressions to communicate feelings *e.g., nods when asked if he is feeling sad*	Identifies and labels own feelings *e.g., says, "I'm mad at you"; "I really want to paint today"*	Is able to describe feelings and their causes *e.g., says, "I'm excited because my dad is coming home"; "I'm mad because they won't let me play with them"*	Is increasingly able to manage own feelings *e.g., calms self down when angry and uses words to explain why; chooses to go to a quiet area to be alone when upset*
4. **Stands up for rights**	**Forerunners** Protests when slighted or wronged by crying or yelling Grabs or pushes when seeking a desired toy	Physically or verbally asserts needs and desires *e.g., continues to hold classroom pet another child wants; lets teacher know if another child refuses to give anyone a turn on the ride-on truck*	Asserts own needs and desires verbally without being aggressive *e.g., says, "It's my turn now" when sand timer runs out; tells friend who asks to paint at the easel, "I'm not done," and continues working*	Takes action to avoid possible disputes over rights *e.g., puts up "Do not knock down" sign in front of block structure; divides sandbox into area for himself and peer*

Responsibility for Self and Others

Developmental Continuum for Ages 3-5

Curriculum Objectives	Forerunners	I	II	III
5. **Demonstrates self-direction and independence**	**Forerunners** Purposefully indicates needs or wants (may be nonverbal) Selects toy or activity; plays briefly	Chooses and becomes involved in one activity out of several options *e.g., during free play decides to play with giant dominoes on floor in toys and games area; after waking up from nap, takes book from shelf in library area and looks at it*	Completes multiple tasks in a project of own choosing with some adult assistance *e.g., makes a collage: collects materials, glue, paper, and scissors and works until done; builds a zoo with blocks, animal and people props, and cars*	Carves out and completes own task without adult assistance *e.g., draws one section of mural without intruding on other sections; makes a book about family trip that includes 5 pictures in sequence*
6. **Takes responsibility for own well-being**	**Forerunners** Allows adult to attend to personal needs such as dressing or washing hands without resistance Uses self-help skills with adult assistance such as brushing teeth or putting on coat with help	Uses self-help skills with occasional reminders *e.g., tries new foods when encouraged by teacher; washes hands with soap and water following procedures taught*	Uses self-help skills and participates in chores without reminders *e.g., goes to get a sponge after spilling juice; helps throw away trash after a picnic*	Understands the importance of self-help skills and their role in healthy living *e.g., tries new foods and talks about what's good for you; knows why it's important to wash hands and brush teeth*
7. **Respects and cares for classroom environment and materials**	**Forerunners** Engages with/explores materials for brief periods of time with adult assistance or independently Participates in clean-up routines when asked	Uses materials in appropriate ways *e.g., paints at easel; turns pages in book carefully without tearing*	Puts away used materials before starting another activity *e.g., shuts off the tape recorder before leaving the listening center; returns puzzle to shelf*	Begins to take responsibility for care of the classroom environment *e.g., gets broom and dust pan to help remove sand; pitches in willingly to move furniture to clear a group area*
8. **Follows classroom routines**	**Forerunners** Allows adult to move him/her through routines Follows classroom routines with assistance such as reminders, picture cues, or physical help	Participates in classroom activities (e.g., circle time, clean-up, napping, toileting, eating, etc.) with prompting *e.g., after cleaning up, goes to rug for circle time when the teacher strums the autoharp*	Understands and follows classroom procedures without prompting *e.g., goes to wash hands and brush teeth after lunch*	Follows and understands the purpose of classroom procedures *e.g., tells peer that he can't eat lunch until he's washed his hands*

Responsibility for Self and Others (continued)

Developmental Continuum for Ages 3-5

Curriculum Objectives	Forerunners	I	II	III
9. **Follows classroom rules**	**Forerunners** Follows simple directions and limits when told by an adult Follows classroom rules with assistance such as reminders, picture cues, or physical help	Follows classroom rules with reminders *e.g., responds positively to guidance such as "speak with your indoor voice"*	Understands and follows classroom rules without reminders *e.g., returns puzzles to shelf before leaving the table area*	Follows and understands reasons for classroom rules *e.g., tells friend to put artwork on shelf so it will be safe; reminds peer not to run in classroom so that no one will get hurt*

Prosocial Behavior

Curriculum Objectives		Developmental Continuum for Ages 3-5		
		I	II	III
10. **Plays well with other children**	Forerunners Tolerates being physically near others Plays alongside another child Enjoys simple back and forth games such as hide and seek	Works/plays cooperatively with one other child e.g., draws or paints beside peer, making occasional comments; has a pretend phone conversation with another child	Successfully enters a group and plays cooperatively e.g., joins other children caring for babies in dramatic play center; plans with peers what they will need to set up a class restaurant	Maintains an ongoing friendship with at least one other child e.g., says, "We're friends again, right?" after working through a conflict; talks about another child as "my best friend"
11. **Recognizes the feelings of others and responds appropriately**	Forerunners Notices expressions of feelings in others e.g., looks or reacts by crying or laughing Imitates other children's expressions of feelings	Is aware of other children's feelings and often responds in a like manner e.g., laughs or smiles when others are happy; says a child is sad because her mom left	Shows increasing awareness that people may have different feelings about the same situation e.g., says that another child is afraid of thunder but, "I'm not"; acts out role of angry parent during pretend play	Recognizes what another person might need or want e.g., brings a book on trucks to show a child who loves trucks; helps a friend who is having difficulty opening a milk carton
12. **Shares and respects the rights of others**	Forerunners Plays alongside another child using same or similar materials with adult assistance Plays alongside another child using same or similar materials without conflict	With prompts, shares or takes turns with others e.g., allows sand timer to regulate turns with favorite toys; complies with teacher's request to let another child have a turn on the tricycle	Shares toys or allows turn in response to another child's request e.g., appropriately occupies self while waiting for others to leave swings without crying or demanding a turn; plays at sand table without grabbing items being used by others	Shares and defends the rights of others to a turn e.g., reminds child who doesn't want to relinquish a turn that it is another child's turn; asks teacher to intervene when two children begin to fight over a toy
13. **Uses thinking skills to resolve conflicts**	Forerunners Accepts adult solution to resolve a conflict Seeks adult assistance to resolve a conflict e.g., cries, approaches adult, or asks for help	Accepts compromise when suggested by peer or teacher e.g., agrees to play with another toy while waiting for a turn; goes to "peace table" with teacher and peer to solve a problem	Suggests a solution to solve a problem; seeks adult assistance when needed e.g., suggests trading one toy for another; asks teacher to make a waiting list for the water table	Engages in a process of negotiation to reach a compromise e.g., works out roles for a dramatic play episode; suggests going to the "peace table" to work out a problem

PHYSICAL DEVELOPMENT

Gross Motor

Curriculum Objectives		Developmental Continuum for Ages 3-5		
		I	II	III
14. **Demonstrates basic locomotor skills (running, jumping, hopping, galloping)**	**Forerunners** Walks with assistance Runs, sometimes falls Jumps and hops with hand held	Moves with direction and beginning coordination *e.g., runs avoiding obstacles; jumps forward, may lead with one foot; hops in place once or twice*	Moves with direction and increasing coordination *e.g., runs moving arms and legs; does a running jump with both feet; attempts to skip, often reverting to galloping*	Moves with direction and refined coordination *e.g., runs quickly changing directions, starting and stopping; jumps forward from standing position; gallops smoothly*
15. **Shows balance while moving**	**Forerunners** Walks on toes Easily stops, starts, changes direction, avoids obstacles Walks forward straddling line	Attempts to walk along a line, stepping off occasionally	Walks along wide beam such as edge of sandbox	Walks forward easily, and backward with effort, along a wide beam
16. **Climbs up and down**	**Forerunners** Crawls up stairs on own Walks up stairs with hand held Climbs a short, wide ladder with support from adult	Climbs a short, wide ladder	Climbs up and down stairs and ladders, and around obstacles	Climbs and plays easily on ramps, stairs, ladders, or sliding boards
17. **Pedals and steers a tricycle (or other wheeled vehicle)**	**Forerunners** Sits on tricycle or other riding toy, pushing forward/backward with feet not using pedals Pedals tricycle, difficulty with steering	Pedals in forward direction, steering around wide corners	Pedals and steers around obstacles and sharp corners	Rides with speed and control

Gross Motor (continued)

Curriculum Objectives	Developmental Continuum for Ages 3-5			
	Forerunners	I	II	III
18. **Demonstrates throwing, kicking, and catching skills**	Hurls beanbag or ball Sits on floor and traps a rolled ball with arms and body Kicks a ball a short distance with hand held to maintain balance	Throws, catches, and kicks objects with somewhat awkward movements *e.g., throws ball with both hands; catches a large ball against body; kicks ball from standing position*	Throws, catches, and kicks with increasing control *e.g., throws ball overhand several feet toward target; catches bounced ball; moves toward ball and kicks*	Throws and kicks at target and catches with increasing accuracy *e.g., throws object with smooth overhand motion; catches object with elbows bent; kicks ball with fluid motion*

Fine Motor

Developmental Continuum for Ages 3-5

Curriculum Objectives		I	II	III
19. **Controls small muscles in hands**	**Forerunners** Uses self-help skills such as: finger feeds self; removes shoes/socks; washes hands with assistance Drops objects into container Touches thumb to finger to pick up object	Manipulates objects with hands *e.g., places large pegs in pegboard; buttons large buttons on own clothes; uses scissors to make snips*	Manipulates smaller objects with increasing control *e.g., eats with a fork; inserts and removes small pegs in pegboard; squeezes clothespin to hang painting; cuts with scissors along a straight or slightly curved line*	Manipulates a variety of objects requiring increased coordination *e.g., creates recognizable objects with clay; buttons, zips, and sometimes ties; cuts with scissors along lines, turning corners; cuts simple shapes out of paper*
20. **Coordinates eye-hand movement**	**Forerunners** Removes pegs from pegboard Opens a board book and turns a page Puts one block on top of another, holding the base block	Performs simple manipulations *e.g., makes a necklace with a string and large beads; rolls and pounds playdough; places pegs in pegboard*	Performs simple manipulations with increasing control *e.g., makes a necklace using small beads; pours water into a funnel*	Manipulates materials in a purposeful way, planning and attending to detail *e.g., strings a variety of small objects (straws, buttons, etc.); using table blocks, creates a tall structure that balances; completes 8-piece puzzle*
21. **Uses tools for writing and drawing**	**Forerunners** Holds large writing tool and marks with it Holds marker in palmar grasp and scribbles	Holds a marker or crayon with thumb and two fingers; makes simple strokes	Makes several basic strokes or figures; draws some recognizable objects	Copies and draws simple shapes, letters, and words including name

100

COGNITIVE DEVELOPMENT

Learning and Problem Solving

Developmental Continuum for Ages 3-5

Curriculum Objectives	Forerunners	I	II	III
22. Observes objects and events with curiosity	**Forerunners** Looks at and touches object presented by an adult or another child Explores materials in the environment *e.g., touching, looking, smelling, mouthing, listening, playing*	Examines with attention to detail, noticing attributes of objects *e.g., points out stripes on caterpillar; notices it gets darker when the sun goes behind a cloud; points out changes in animals or plants in room*	Notices and/or asks questions about similarities and differences *e.g., points out that two trucks are the same size; asks why the leaves fall off the trees*	Observes attentively and seeks relevant information *e.g., describes key features of different models of cars (such as logos, number of doors, type of license plate); investigates which objects will sink and which will float*
23. Approaches problems flexibly	**Forerunners** Imitates adult or peer in solving problems Repeats and persists in trial and error approach	Finds multiple uses for classroom objects *e.g., uses wooden blocks as musical instruments; strings wooden beads into necklace for dress-up*	Experiments with materials in new ways when first way doesn't work *e.g., when playdough recipe produces sticky dough, asks for more flour; fills plastic bottle with water to make it sink*	Finds alternative solutions to problems *e.g., suggests using block as doorstop when classroom doorstop disappears; offers to swap trike for riding toy she wants and then adds firefighter hat to the bargain*
24. Shows persistence in approaching tasks	**Forerunners** Remains engaged in a task for short periods with assistance Stays involved in self-selected activity such as playing with playdough for short periods	Sees simple tasks through to completion *e.g., puts toys away before going on to next activity; completes 5-piece puzzle*	Continues to work on task even when encountering difficulties *e.g., rebuilds block tower when it tumbles; keeps trying different puzzle pieces when pieces aren't fitting together*	Works on task over time, leaving and returning to complete it *e.g., continues to work on Lego structure over 3-day period; creates grocery store out of hollow blocks, adding more detail each day, and involves other children in playing grocery*
25. Explores cause and effect	**Forerunners** Notices an effect *e.g., shows pleasure in turning light switch on and off, wants to do it again; repeatedly stacks blocks and watches them fall* Looks for something when it is out of sight	Notices and comments on effect *e.g., while shaking a jar of water says, "Look at the bubbles when I do this"; after spinning around and stopping says, "Spinning makes the room look like it's moving up and down"*	Wonders "what will happen if" and tests out possibilities *e.g., blows into cardboard tubes of different sizes to hear if different sounds are made; changes the incline of a board to make cars slide down faster*	Explains plans for testing cause and effect, and tries out ideas *e.g., places pennies one by one in 2 floating boats ("I'm seeing which boat sinks first"); mixes gray paint to match another batch ("Let's put in one drop of white at a time 'til it's right")*

Learning and Problem Solving (continued)

Developmental Continuum for Ages 3-5

Curriculum Objectives	Forerunners	I	II	III
26. **Applies knowledge or experience to a new context**	Follows familiar self-help routines at school (toileting, eating)—may need assistance	Draws on everyday experiences and applies this knowledge to similar situations *e.g., washes hands after playing at sand table; rocks baby doll in arms*	Applies new information or vocabulary to an activity or interaction *e.g., comments, "We're bouncing like Tigger" when jumping up and down with peer; uses traffic-directing signals after seeing a police officer demonstrate them*	Generates a rule, strategy, or idea from one learning experience and applies it in a new context *e.g., after learning to access one computer program by clicking on icons, uses similar procedures to access others; suggests voting to resolve a classroom issue*

Logical Thinking

Developmental Continuum for Ages 3-5

Curriculum Objectives		I	II	III
27. **Classifies objects**	**Forerunners** Finds two objects that are the same and comments or puts them together Groups similar kinds of toys together such as cars, blocks, or dolls	Sorts objects by one property such as size, shape, color, or use *e.g., sorts pebbles into three buckets by color; puts square block with other square blocks*	Sorts a group of objects by one property and then by another *e.g., collects leaves and sorts by size and then by color; puts self in group wearing shoes that tie and then in group with blue shoes*	Sorts objects into groups/subgroups and can state reason *e.g., sorts stickers into four piles ("Here are the stars that are silver and gold, and here are circles, silver and gold"); piles animals and then divides them into zoo and farm animals*
28. **Compares/ measures**	**Forerunners** Notices something new or different *e.g., a new classmate or a new toy on the shelf* Notices similarities of objects *e.g., "We have the same shoes"*	Notices similarities and differences *e.g., states, "The rose is the only flower in our garden that smells"; "I can run fast in my new shoes"*	Uses comparative words related to number, size, shape, texture, weight, color, speed, volume *e.g., "This bucket is heavier than that one"; "Now the music is going faster"*	Understands/uses measurement words and some standard measurement tools *e.g., uses unit blocks to measure length of rug; "We need 2 cups of flour and 1 cup of salt to make dough"*
29. **Arranges objects in a series**	**Forerunners** Uses self-correcting toys such as form boards and graduated stacking rings Sorts by one attribute *e.g., big blocks and little blocks*	Notices when one object in a series is out of place *e.g., removes the one measuring spoon out of place in a line and tries to put it in right place*	Figures out a logical order for a group of objects *e.g., makes necklace of graduated wooden beads; arranges magazine pictures of faces from nicest expression to meanest*	Through trial and error, arranges objects along a continuum according to two or more physical features *e.g., lines up bottle caps by height and width; sorts playdough cookies by size, color, and shape*
30. **Recognizes patterns and can repeat them**	**Forerunners** Completes a sentence that repeats in a familiar story Hums, sings, or responds to a chorus that repeats in a familiar song Completes a simple form board	Notices and recreates simple patterns with objects *e.g., makes a row of blocks alternating in size (big-small-big-small); strings beads in repeating patterns of 2 colors*	Extends patterns or creates simple patterns of own design *e.g., makes necklace of beads in which a sequence of 2 or more colors is repeated; continues block pattern of 2 colors*	Creates complex patterns of own design or by copying *e.g., imitates hand-clapping pattern (long clap followed by 3 short claps); designs a 3-color pattern using colored inch cubes and repeats it across the table*

Logical Thinking (continued)

Developmental Continuum for Ages 3-5

Curriculum Objectives	Forerunners	I	II	III
31. Shows awareness of time concepts and sequence	Follows steps in simple routine such as in dressing or at naptime Demonstrates understanding of what comes next in daily schedule *e.g., goes to the table anticipating mealtime*	Demonstrates understanding of the present and may refer to past and future *e.g., responds appropriately when asked, "What did you do this morning?"; talks about, "Later, when Mom comes to pick me up"*	Uses past and future tenses and time words appropriately *e.g., talks about tomorrow, yesterday, last week; says, "After work time, we go outside"*	Associates events with time-related concepts *e.g., "Tomorrow is Saturday so there's no school"; "My birthday was last week"; "I go to bed at night"*
32. Shows awareness of position in space	Moves objects from one container to another Follows simple positional directions with assistance *e.g., puts paper in trash can*	Shows comprehension of basic positional words and concepts *e.g., puts object in, on, under, on top of, or next to another object as requested*	Understands and uses positional words correctly *e.g., "Come sit near me"; "The fish food goes on the top shelf"*	Shows understanding that positional relationships vary with one's perspective *e.g., turns lotto card around so player opposite him can see it right side up; "I can reach the ring when I'm on the top step, but from here it's too far"*
33. Uses one-to-one correspondence	Places an object in each designated space *e.g., puts a peg doll in each hole in a toy bus*	Matches pairs of objects in one-to-one correspondence *e.g., searches through dress-ups to find two shoes for her feet*	Places objects in one-to-one correspondence with another set *e.g., lines up brushes to make sure there is one for each jar of paint; goes around the table placing one cup at each child's place*	Uses one-to-one correspondence as a way to compare two sets *e.g., lines up cubes across from a friend's row to determine who has more; puts one rider next to each horse saying, "Are there enough horses for all the cowboys?"*
34. Uses numbers and counting	Understands the concept of "one" *e.g., picks up one object when asked* Understands the concept of more *e.g., picks up more of something when directed, or asks for more cheese*	Imitates counting behavior using number names (may not always say one number per item or get the sequence right) *e.g., says the numbers from 1 to 5 while moving finger along a row of 8 items (not realizing that counting means one number per item)*	Counts correctly up to 5 or so using one number for each object (may not always keep track of what has or has not been counted) *e.g., counts out 5 pretzels taking one at a time from bowl; counts a collection of objects but may count an object more than one time*	Counts to 10 or so connecting number words and symbols to the objects counted and knows that the last number describes the total *e.g., counts 8 bottle caps and says, "I have 8"; spins dial, then moves board game piece 6 spaces; draws 5 figures to show members of family*

Representation and Symbolic Thinking

Developmental Continuum for Ages 3-5

Curriculum Objectives		I	II	III
35. **Takes on pretend roles and situations**	**Forerunners** Imitates simple action *e.g., picks up phone; rocks baby* With adult or peer support, imitates routines *e.g., pretends to feed doll; pours coffee; pretends to sleep*	Performs and labels actions associated with a role *e.g., feeding the baby doll, says, "I'm the Mommy"; picks up phone and says, "Hello, is Suzie there?"*	Offers a play theme and scenario *e.g., "Let's play school"; while listening to doll's heartbeat with stethoscope announces that it's time to get the baby to the hospital*	Engages in elaborate and sustained role play *e.g., suggests a play theme and discusses who will do what; discusses with peer what to buy at grocery store, takes pocketbook and goes to grocery store*
36. **Makes believe with objects**	**Forerunners** Imitates adult's or another child's use of familiar objects *e.g., rocks doll; stirs the pot* Interacts appropriately with objects with adult or peer support *e.g., responds to pretend phone call by putting phone to ear and vocalizing*	Interacts appropriately with real objects or replicas in pretend play *e.g., uses a broken phone to make a pretend phone call; puts playdough cookies on little plastic plates*	Uses substitute object or gesture to represent real object *e.g., holds hand to ear and pretends to dial phone; builds a sand castle and puts shell on top for "satellite dish"*	Uses make-believe props in planned and sustained play *e.g., pretends with a peer to be garage mechanics working on cars made of blocks; sets up scene for playing school—students sit on pillows and teacher has a box for a desk*
37. **Makes and interprets representations**	**Forerunners** Labels scribbles as people or common objects Interacts and builds with blocks Begins to use descriptive labels in construction play *e.g., "house," "road"*	Draws or constructs and then names what it is *e.g., draws pictures with different shapes and says, "This is my house"; lines up unit blocks and says, "I'm making a road"*	Draws or builds a construction that represents something specific *e.g., makes a helicopter with Bristle Blocks; draws 6 legs on insect after looking at beetle*	Plans then creates increasingly elaborate representations *e.g., uses blocks to make a maze for the class gerbil; draws fire truck and includes many details*

LANGUAGE DEVELOPMENT

Listening and Speaking

Curriculum Objectives		Developmental Continuum for Ages 3-5		
		I	II	III
38. Hears and discriminates the sounds of language	**Forerunners** Notices sounds in the environment *e.g., pays attention to birds singing, sirens* Joins in nursery rhymes and songs	Plays with words, sounds, and rhymes *e.g., repeats songs, rhymes, and chants; says, "Oh you Silly Willy"*	Recognizes and invents rhymes and repetitive phrases; notices words that begin the same way *e.g., makes up silly rhymes ("Bo, Bo, Biddle, Bop"); says, "My name begins the same as pop-corn and pig"*	Hears and repeats separate sounds in words; plays with sounds to create new words *e.g., claps hands 3 times when saying "Su-zan-na"; says, "Pass the bapkin [napkin]"*
39. Expresses self using words and expanded sentences	**Forerunners** Uses non-verbal gestures or single words to communicate *e.g., points to ball* Uses 2-word phrases *e.g., "All gone"; "Go out"*	Uses simple sentences (3-4 words) to express wants and needs *e.g., "I want the trike"*	Uses longer sentences (5-6 words) to communicate *e.g., "I want to ride the trike when we go outside"*	Uses more complex sentences to express ideas and feelings *e.g., "I hope we can go outside today because I want to ride the tricycle around the track"*
40. Understands and follows oral directions	**Forerunners** Associates words with actions *e.g., says "throw" when sees ball thrown; throws when hears the word* Follows oral directions when combined with gestures *e.g., "come here" accompanied with gesture*	Follows one-step directions *e.g., "Please get a tissue"*	Follows two-step directions *e.g., "When you get inside, please hang up your coat"*	Follows directions with more than two steps *e.g., follows directions to put clay in container, wipe table, and wash hands when activity is finished*
41. Answers questions	**Forerunners** Answers yes/no questions with words, gestures, or signs *e.g., points to purple paint when asked what color she wants*	Answers simple questions with one or two words *e.g., when asked for name says, "Curtis"; says, "Purple and blue" when asked the colors of paint*	Answers questions with a complete thought *e.g., responds, "I took a bus to school"; "I want purple and blue paint"*	Answers questions with details *e.g., describes a family trip when asked about weekend; says, "I want purple and blue like my new shoes so I can make lots of flowers"*

Developmental Continuum for Ages 3-5

Curriculum Objectives	Forerunners	I	II	III
42. **Asks questions**	**Forerunners** Uses facial expressions/ gestures to ask a question Uses rising intonation to ask questions *e.g., "Mama comes back?"* Uses some "wh" words (what and where) to ask questions *e.g., "What that?"*	Asks simple questions *e.g., "What's for lunch?" "Can we play outside today?"*	Asks questions to further understanding *e.g., "Where did the snow go when it melted?" "Why does that man wear a uniform?"*	Asks increasingly complex questions to further own understanding *e.g., "What happened to the water in the fish tank? Did the fish drink it?"*
43. **Actively participates in conversations**	**Forerunners** Initiates communication by smiling and/or eye contact Responds to social greetings *e.g., waves in response to "hello" or "bye-bye"*	Responds to comments and questions from others *e.g., when one child says, "I have new shoes," shows own shoes and says, "Look at my new shoes"*	Responds to others' comments in a series of exchanges *e.g., makes relevant comments during a group discussion; provides more information when message is not understood*	Initiates and/or extends conversations for at least four exchanges *e.g., while talking with a friend, asks questions about what happened, what friend did, and shares own ideas*

Reading and Writing

Developmental Continuum for Ages 3-5

Curriculum Objectives		I	II	III
44. **Enjoys and values reading**	**Forerunners** Looks at books and pictures with an adult or another child Chooses and looks at books independently Completes phrases in familiar stories	Listens to stories being read *e.g., asks teacher to read favorite story; repeats refrain when familiar book is read aloud*	Participates in story time interactively *e.g., answers questions before, during, and after read-aloud session; relates story to self; acts out familiar story with puppets*	Chooses to read on own; seeks information in books; sees self as reader *e.g., gives reasons for liking a book; looks for other books by favorite author; uses book on birds to identify egg found on nature walk*
45. **Demonstrates understanding of print concepts**	**Forerunners** Points to print on page and says, "Read this" Recognizes logos *e.g., McDonald's* Recognizes book by cover	Knows that print carries the message *e.g., points to printed label on shelf and says, "Cars go here"; looking at the name the teacher has written on another child's drawing, says, "Whose is this?"*	Shows general knowledge of how print works *e.g., runs finger over text left to right, top to bottom as he pretends to read; knows that names begin with a big letter*	Knows each spoken word can be written down and read *e.g., touches a written word for every spoken word in a story; looking at a menu asks, "Which word says pancakes?"*
46. **Demonstrates knowledge of the alphabet**	**Forerunners** Participates in songs and fingerplays about letters Points out print in environment *e.g., name on cubby, exit sign*	Recognizes and identifies a few letters by name *e.g., points to a cereal box and says, "That's C like in my name"*	Recognizes and names many letters *e.g., uses alphabet stamps and names the letters— "D, T, M"*	Beginning to make letter-sound connections *e.g., writes a big M and says, "This is for Mommy"*
47. **Uses emerging reading skills to make meaning from print**	**Forerunners** Uses familiar logos and words to read print *e.g., cereal logos, "exit" and "stop" signs* Recognizes own name in print and uses it as a cue to find possessions *e.g., cubby, cot, placemat*	Uses illustrations to guess what the text says *e.g., looking at The Three Pigs, says, "And the wolf blew down the pig's house"*	Makes judgements about words and text by noticing features (other than letters or words) *e.g., "That must be Christopher's name because it's so long"; "You didn't write enough words. I said, 'A Book about the Dog Biff,' and you just wrote three words"*	Uses different strategies (known words, knowledge of letters and sounds, patterns in text) to make meaning from print *e.g., "That word says book"; anticipates what comes next based on pattern in Brown Bear; figures out which word says banana because he knows it starts with b*

Reading and Writing (continued)

Developmental Continuum for Ages 3-5

Curriculum Objectives		I	II	III
48. **Comprehends and interprets meaning from books and other texts**	**Forerunners** Repeats words and actions demonstrated in books *e.g., roars like a lion* Relates story to self and shares information *e.g., after hearing a story about snow says, "I made a snowman"*	Imitates act of reading in play *e.g., holds up book and pretends to read to baby doll; takes out phonebook in dramatic play area to make a phone call*	Compares and predicts story events; acts out main events of a familiar story *e.g., compares own feelings about baby brother to those of character; re-enacts Three Billy Goats Gruff*	Retells a story including many details and draws connections between story events *e.g., says, "The wolf blew the house down because it wasn't strong"; uses flannel board to retell The Very Hungry Caterpillar*
49. **Understands the purpose of writing**	**Forerunners** Watches when others write Pretends to write *(scribble writes)*	Imitates act of writing in play *e.g., pretends to write a prescription while playing clinic; scribble writes next to a picture*	Understands there is a way to write that conveys meaning *e.g., tells teacher, "Write this down so everyone can read it"; asks teacher, "How do I write Happy Birthday?"; says, "That's not writing, that's scribble-scrabble"*	Writes to convey meaning *e.g., on drawing for sick friend, writes own name; copies teacher's sign, "Do Not Disturb," to put near block pattern; makes deliberate letter choices during writing attempts*
50. **Writes letters and words**	**Forerunners** Scribbles with crayons Experiments with writing tools such as markers and pencils Draws simple pictures to represent something	Uses scribble writing and letter-like forms	Writes recognizable letters, especially those in own name	Uses letters that represent sounds in writing words

109

Appendix C

Additional Gross Motor Skills
A Further Breakdown of Objectives 14 and 18

*This is an optional tool for programs that
wish more detailed information*

Physical Development

Additional Gross Motor Skills

(A Further Breakdown of Objectives 14 and 18)

Developmental Continuum for Ages 3-5

Curriculum Objectives		I	II	III
Develops and refines running skills	**Forerunners** Walks with assistance; walks independently; walks, avoiding obstacles Runs, sometimes falls	Runs with direction, avoiding obstacles	Runs smoothly, with speed, moving arms reciprocally with legs	Runs quickly, changing directions, starting and stopping easily
Develops and refines jumping skills	**Forerunners** Jumps with hand held Jumps in place with both feet landing together	Jumps off a step and lands with both feet; jumps forward, may lead with one foot	Does a running broad jump with both feet together	From standing position, jumps forward several feet with both feet together
Develops and refines galloping skills	**Forerunners** Walks quickly with consistent pace and direction Varies pace while walking and running	Attempts to gallop a few paces, leading with one foot	Gallops a few feet forward, reverts to running after several steps	Gallops smoothly and with directions for a short distance
Develops and refines hopping skills	**Forerunners** Stands on one foot with hand held Hops with hand held Hops in place on one foot one time	Hops in place on one foot at least two consecutive times	Hops forward on one foot a distance of several feet	Hops forward on one foot across playground

112

Additional Gross Motor Skills (continued)

Curriculum Objectives	Developmental Continuum for Ages 3-5			
	Forerunners	I	II	III
Develops and refines throwing skills	**Forerunners** Grasps beanbag or ball but can't release object Hurls beanbag or ball	Throws a ball several feet toward a person or target, either overhand or underhand	Throws a ball overhand several feet toward a person or target, following through with arm	Throws a ball a short distance toward a person or target with accuracy
Develops and refines catching skills	**Forerunners** Engages in ball play Sits on floor in straddle position and traps a rolled ball with arms and body	Catches a large ball, standing still and holding arms out straight	Catches a ball with arms in front of body and elbows bent; may trap ball against body	Catches a large ball with arms at side of body and elbows bent
Develops and refines kicking skills	**Forerunners** Walks up to ball and makes contact with foot Kicks a ball a short distance with hand held to maintain balance	Kicks a ball a short distance, maintaining balance	Runs toward a ball and kicks it a short distance with direction	Kicks a ball several feet in the air toward a target

Appendix D

Applying Content Standards to Your Program Requirements

How the Components of Literacy Are Addressed in *The Creative Curriculum*®

COMPONENTS	REQUIREMENTS FOR YOUR PROGRAM	*CREATIVE CURRICULUM* OBJECTIVES
Increased Vocabulary and Language (Acquires new words and uses them to communicate)		3. Recognizes own feelings and manages them appropriately 38. Hears and discriminates the sounds of language 39. Expresses self using words and expanded sentences 40. Understands and follows oral directions 41. Answers questions 42. Asks questions 43. Actively participates in conversations
Phonological Awareness (Hears and discriminates the sounds of spoken words; recognizes words that sound the same and words that sound different)		38. Hears and discriminates the sounds of language 46. Demonstrates knowledge of the alphabet 50. Writes letters and words
Understanding Books and Other Texts (Learns how to use a book and the purpose of books; gains a sense of story; learns about the uses of other texts such as signs, menus, magazines, newspapers, etc.)		44. Enjoys and values reading 45. Demonstrates understanding of print concepts 47. Uses emerging reading skills to make meaning from print 48. Comprehends and interprets meaning from books and other texts 50. Writes letters and words

TEACHING STRATEGIES

Permission is granted to duplicate for use in programs implementing *The Creative Curriculum*® *for Early Childhood.*

How the Components of Literacy Are Addressed in *The Creative Curriculum*®

COMPONENTS	REQUIREMENTS FOR YOUR PROGRAM	*CREATIVE CURRICULUM* OBJECTIVES
Knowledge of Print (Learns how print works)		45. Demonstrates understanding of print concepts 46. Demonstrates knowledge of the alphabet 47. Uses emerging reading skills to make meaning from print 48. Comprehends and interprets meaning from books and other texts 49. Understands the purpose of writing 50. Writes letters and words
Letters and Words (Identifies and writes some letters and words)		21. Uses tools for writing and drawing 37. Makes and interprets representations 46. Demonstrates knowledge of the alphabet 47. Uses emerging reading skills to make meaning from print 49. Understands the purpose of writing 50. Writes letters and words
Comprehension (Understands and follows what is going on in a book, story, or conversation)		44. Enjoys and values reading 45. Demonstrates understanding of print concepts 47. Uses emerging reading skills to make meaning from print 48. Comprehends and interprets meaning from books and other texts
Literacy as a Source of Enjoyment (Enjoys being read to and reading and writing)		35. Takes on pretend roles and situations 38. Hears and discriminates the sounds of language 44. Enjoys and values reading 45. Demonstrates understanding of print concepts 47. Uses emerging reading skills to make meaning from print 48. Comprehends and interprets meaning from books and other texts

TEACHING STRATEGIES

Permission is granted to duplicate for use in programs implementing *The Creative Curriculum*® for Early Childhood.

How the Components of Math Are Addressed in *The Creative Curriculum®*

COMPONENTS	REQUIREMENTS FOR YOUR PROGRAM	*CREATIVE CURRICULUM* OBJECTIVES
Number Concepts (Understands numbers, ways of representing numbers, and relationships between numbers)		22. Observes objects and events with curiosity 23. Approaches problems flexibly 28. Compares/measures 33. Uses one-to-one correspondence 34. Uses numbers and counting
Patterns and Relationships (Recognizes, copies, extends patterns; makes predictions about patterns in the environment)		22. Observes objects and events with curiosity 23. Approaches problems flexibly 27. Classifies objects 28. Compares/measures 30. Recognizes patterns and can repeat them 37. Makes and interprets representations
Geometry and Spatial Sense (Recognizes, names, builds, draws, describes, compares, and sorts two- and three-dimensional shapes; recognizes and describes spatial relationships)		22. Observes objects and events with curiosity 23. Approaches problems flexibly 27. Classifies objects 28. Compares/measures 32. Shows awareness of position in space 37. Makes and interprets representations

TEACHING STRATEGIES INC.

Permission is granted to duplicate for use in programs implementing *The Creative Curriculum® for Early Childhood.*

How the Components of Math Are Addressed in *The Creative Curriculum*®

COMPONENTS	REQUIREMENTS FOR YOUR PROGRAM	*CREATIVE CURRICULUM* OBJECTIVES
Measurement (Uses non-standard units to measure and make comparisons)		22. Observes objects and events with curiosity 23. Approaches problems flexibly 27. Classifies objects 28. Compares/measures 29. Arranges objects in a series 31. Shows awareness of time concepts and sequence 34. Uses numbers and counting
Data Collection, Organization, and Representation (Poses questions to investigate, organizes responses, and creates representations of data)		22. Observes objects and events with curiosity 23. Approaches problems flexibly 27. Classifies objects 28. Compares/measures 29. Arranges objects in a series 30. Recognizes patterns and can repeat them 33. Uses one-to-one correspondence 34. Uses numbers and counting 37. Makes and interprets representations

TEACHING STRATEGIES

Permission is granted to duplicate for use in programs implementing *The Creative Curriculum*® *for Early Childhood.*

How the Components of Science Are Addressed in *The Creative Curriculum*®

COMPONENTS	REQUIREMENTS FOR YOUR PROGRAM	*CREATIVE CURRICULUM* OBJECTIVES
Physical Science (Explores the physical properties of the world by observing and manipulating common objects and materials in the environment)		22. Observes objects and events with curiosity 25. Explores cause and effect 27. Classifies objects 28. Compares/measures 29. Arranges objects in a series 30. Recognizes patterns and can repeat them 32. Shows awareness of position in space
Life Science (Explores living things, their life cycles, and their habitats)		7. Respects and cares for classroom environment and materials 12. Shares and respects the rights of others 22. Observes objects and events with curiosity 25. Explores cause and effect 31. Shows awareness of time concepts and sequence
Earth and the Environment (Explores the properties of the world around them, notices changes, and makes predictions)		7. Respects and cares for classroom environment and materials 25. Explores cause and effect 27. Classifies objects 28. Compares/measures 31. Shows awareness of time concepts and sequence 32. Shows awareness of position in space

TEACHING STRATEGIES

Permission is granted to duplicate for use in programs implementing *The Creative Curriculum*® *for Early Childhood.*

How the Components of Social Studies Are Addressed in *The Creative Curriculum®*

COMPONENTS	REQUIREMENTS FOR YOUR PROGRAM	*CREATIVE CURRICULUM* OBJECTIVES
Spatial or Geographic Thinking (Learns about the physical world around us and how we move about the world)		22. Observes objects and events with curiosity 23. Approaches problems flexibly 25. Explores cause and effect 32. Shows awareness of position in space 37. Makes and interprets representations
People and How They Live (Recognizes and respects likenesses and differences in people; recognizes how people rely on each other for goods and services; learns social skills; understands the need for rules)		1. Shows ability to adjust to new situations 3. Recognizes own feelings and manages them appropriately 4. Stands up for rights 9. Follows classroom rules 10. Plays well with other children 11. Recognizes the feelings of others and responds appropriately 12. Shares and respects the rights of others 13. Uses thinking skills to resolve conflicts
People and the Environment (Learns how people affect the environment by changing it and protecting it)		7. Respects and cares for classroom environment and materials 22. Observes objects and events with curiosity 23. Approaches problems flexibly 25. Explores cause and effect
People and the Past (Learns about how things and people change over time)		22. Observes objects and events with curiosity 25. Explores cause and effect 29. Arranges objects in a series 31. Shows awareness of time concepts and sequence 35. Takes on pretend roles and situations

TEACHING STRATEGIES

Permission is granted to duplicate for use in programs implementing *The Creative Curriculum®* for Early Childhood.

How the Components of Arts Are Addressed in *The Creative Curriculum*®

COMPONENTS	REQUIREMENTS FOR YOUR PROGRAM	*CREATIVE CURRICULUM* OBJECTIVES
Dance (Learns about the body's ability to move and use time and space in different ways)		3. Recognizes own feelings and manages them appropriately 14. Demonstrates basic locomotor skills (running, jumping, hopping, galloping) 15. Shows balance while moving 30. Recognizes patterns and can repeat them 35. Takes on pretend roles and situations 37. Makes and interprets representations 40. Understands and follows oral directions
Music (Develops an awareness of different kinds of music and becomes comfortable with different forms of musical expression)		3. Recognizes own feelings and manages them appropriately 25. Explores cause and effect 30. Recognizes patterns and can repeat them 31. Shows awareness of time concepts and sequence 34. Uses numbers and counting 35. Takes on pretend roles and situations 38. Hears and discriminates the sounds of language 39. Expresses self using words and expanded sentences 40. Understands and follows oral directions
Theater (Communicates a message or story through action or dialogue)		3. Recognizes own feelings and manages them appropriately 11. Recognizes the feelings of others and responds appropriately 22. Observes objects and events with curiosity 31. Shows awareness of time concepts and sequence 32. Shows awareness of position in space 35. Takes on pretend roles and situations 38. Hears and discriminates the sounds of language 39. Expresses self using words and expanded sentences 40. Understands and follows oral directions

TEACHING STRATEGIES

Permission is granted to duplicate for use in programs implementing *The Creative Curriculum*® for Early Childhood.

How the Components of Arts Are Addressed in *The Creative Curriculum*®

COMPONENTS	REQUIREMENTS FOR YOUR PROGRAM	*CREATIVE CURRICULUM* OBJECTIVES
Visual Arts (Uses a variety of media for communication and expression; solves problems using art materials; appreciates many forms of art)		3. Recognizes own feelings and manages them appropriately 7. Respects and cares for classroom environment and materials 19. Controls small muscles in hands 21. Uses tools for writing and drawing 22. Observes objects and events with curiosity 25. Explores cause and effect 30. Recognizes patterns and can repeat them 32. Shows awareness of position in space 37. Makes and interprets representations

TEACHING STRATEGIES

Permission is granted to duplicate for use in programs implementing *The Creative Curriculum*® *for Early Childhood.*

How the Components of Technology Are Addressed in *The Creative Curriculum*®

COMPONENTS	REQUIREMENTS FOR YOUR PROGRAM	*CREATIVE CURRICULUM* OBJECTIVES
Awareness of Technology (Gains awareness of technology as a tool for finding information, communicating, and creating)		22. Observes objects and events with curiosity 35. Takes on pretend roles and situations 36. Makes believe with objects 39. Expresses self using words and expanded sentences 42. Asks questions
Basic Operations and Concepts (Learns basic skills to operate technology; uses appropriate terminology to communicate about technology)		5. Demonstrates self-direction and independence 7. Respects and cares for classroom environment and materials 19. Controls small muscles in hands 22. Observes objects and events with curiosity 23. Approaches problems flexibly 25. Explores cause and effect 37. Makes and interprets representations 46. Demonstrates knowledge of the alphabet 47. Uses emerging reading skills to make meaning from print
Technology Tools (Understands that there are different tools of technology, and they can be used in a variety of ways)		22. Observes objects and events with curiosity 23. Approaches problems flexibly 25. Explores cause and effect 26. Applies knowledge or experience to a new context 36. Makes believe with objects
People and Technology (Understands that technology is controlled by people; uses technology safely and responsibly; works collaboratively while using technology)		5. Demonstrates self-direction and independence 22. Observes objects and events with curiosity 23. Approaches problems flexibly 25. Explores cause and effect 26. Applies knowledge or experience to a new context

TEACHING STRATEGIES

Permission is granted to duplicate for use in programs implementing *The Creative Curriculum*® for Early Childhood.